The Hoover
Commissions Revisited

Westview Replica Editions

The concept of Westview Replica Editions is a response to the continuing crisis in academic and informational publishing. Library budgets for books have been severely curtailed. Ever larger portions of general library budgets are being diverted from the purchase of books and used for data banks, computers, micromedia, and other methods of information retrieval. Interlibrary loan structures further reduce the edition sizes required to satisfy the needs of the scholarly community. Economic pressures (particularly inflation and high interest rates) on the university presses and the few private scholarly publishing companies have severely limited the capacity of the industry to properly serve the academic and research communities. As a result, many manuscripts dealing with important subjects, often representing the highest level of scholarship, are no longer economically viable publishing projects--or, if accepted for publication, are typically subject to lead times ranging from one to three years.

Westview Replica Editions are our practical solution to the problem. We accept a manuscript in camera-ready form, typed according to our specifications, and move it immediately into the production process. As always, the selection criteria include the importance of the subject, the work's contribution to scholarship, and its insight, originality of thought, and excellence of exposition. The responsibility for editing and proofreading lies with the author or sponsoring institution. We prepare chapter headings and display pages, file for copyright, and obtain Library of Congress Cataloging in Publication Data. A detailed manual contains simple instructions for preparing the final typescript, and our editorial staff is always available to answer questions.

The end result is a book printed on acid-free paper and bound in sturdy library-quality soft covers. We manufacture these books ourselves using equipment that does not require a lengthy make-ready process and that allows us to publish first editions of 300 to 600 copies and to reprint even smaller quantities as needed. Thus, we can produce Replica Editions quickly and can keep even very specialized books in print as long as there is a demand for them.

About the Book and Author

The Hoover Commissions Revisited
Ronald C. Moe

In recent years numerous bills have been introduced in Congress to establish a major study effort patterned after the two Hoover Commissions of some thirty years ago. The continuing interest in creating a "new Hoover Commission" has prompted questions about the earlier efforts to restructure national government. What were the Hoover Commissions? How were they structured, and how did they function? What administrative philosophy, if any, guided their work? And what did they accomplish and where did they fail?

This book provides the first detailed analysis of the Hoover Commissions and examines their relevance to recent attempts to initiate government reorganization. Dr. Moe begins with a review of the commissions and their task forces as political institutions and discusses the efforts that were made to generate political support for their recommendations. He then analyzes the impact of the commissions on the presidency, emphasizing that they operated at a time when government agencies were more directly managed by the president --a responsibility now shared by Congress and the Courts. Although the study is historical in perspective, the author ties the experience of the commissions to contemporary political and administrative trends, providing an essential analysis for anyone concerned with making the operation of the federal government more efficient.

Dr. Ronald C. Moe is a specialist in government organization and administration for the Congressional Research Service of the U.S. Library of Congress. He has taught political science at various universities and has held positions in the Department of Commerce, the Department of Health, Education, and Welfare, and the Office of Economic Opportunity. Prior to his current appointment, he was senior policy advisor on the Cost of Living Council in the Executive Office of the president.

Published in cooperation with the
National Academy of Public Administration

The Hoover Commissions Revisited

Ronald C. Moe

Westview Press / Boulder, Colorado

A Westview Replica Edition

Copyright © 1982 by Westview Press, Inc.

Published in 1982 in the United States of America by
    Westview Press, Inc.
    5500 Central Avenue
    Boulder, Colorado 80301
    Frederick A. Praeger, President and Publisher

Library of Congress Cataloging in Publication Data
Moe, Ronald C.
    The Hoover Commissions revisited.
    (A Westview replica edition)
    Bibliography: p.
    1. United States. Commission on Organization of the Executive Branch
of the Government (1947-1949). 2. United States. Commission on Organization
of the Executive Branch of the Government (1953-1955). I. Title.
JK643.C47M6 1982   353'.073   82-10889
ISBN 0-86531-926-X

Printed and bound in the United States of America

10   9   8   7   6   5   4   3   2

Contents

Preface

This is a book about two related study commissions. Called
the first and second Hoover Commissions, after the Chairman, former President Herbert Hoover, these Commissions were unusual in many
respects, not the least being the broad scope of their mandate and
the makeup of the membership. They met in the period following
World War II (first Commission, 1947-49; second Commission, 1953-55)
and attained a high degree of public visibility. They were generally rated as a "success" by the media, although this accolade, when
subjected to analysis, is usually, and more appropriately, reserved
for the first rather than the second Commission.

The Hoover Commissions have not been forgotten. It is a rare
Congress that does not have one or more bills introduced to establish
a "new Hoover Commission." The 97th Congress is no exception. At
the time of this writing, a bill (S. 10) has passed the Senate that
would create a Commission on More Effective Government patterned after the earlier Hoover Commissions. It would have eighteen members,
partly appointed by the President and partly by the leadership of
Congress, "to examine the performance of our Nation's public institutions and to make recommendations for change."

Following two years of study the Commission would submit recommendations ("a blueprint for better government") designed to improve
"the management, operation, and organization of the executive branch"
and the "relationship between the Federal executive branch and State
and local governments." If this sounds like a broad mandate to assign a temporary commission, it is. But the sponsors of the Commission bill are confident that the task is achievable and cite the experience of the two Hoover Commissions thirty years ago to prove
their point. 1/

This is not a book about study commissions in general. There
are numerous types of study commissions, e.g., presidential study
commissions, each with their own characteristics and history. In a
sense, this is a case study rather than an exercise in learning what
is typical about study commissions.

Considering the acknowledged importance of study commissions as actors in our political system, there is relatively little political science literature on the subject. There are several major books and a scattering of articles. 2/ With respect to detailed case studies of major individual commissions, there are none. Most of what was written on the Hoover Commissions, for instance, was written within a couple of years of their conclusion and reflect the dominant political values of the time. 3/ More recently, however, with the opening of the Hoover Presidential Library in West Branch, Iowa, scholars have been given access to additional sources and a reassessment has begun on Mr. Hoover and the Commissions he chaired. 4/

From the outset this author faced two problems. First, whether to present the reader very condensed accounts of all the reports of both Commissions, or a general summary incorporating the highlights of the several reports. Secondly, whether to attempt to survey the Commissions and their reports from the perspective of the time in which they were written or the 1980s. In both instances, I have compromised.

For the most part, each of the reports is summarized separately. The exception occurs with the second Commission for which a number of individual reports are considered together because the recommendations were particularly narrow in scope and relate to problems of that specific period. With respect to the time perspective of this study, it is based principally upon the period in which the reports were written with occasional commentary in the text and footnotes to inform the reader of the subsequent fate of the recommendations each Commission made.

This book is organized around several questions. What were the two Hoover Commissions? How were they structured, and how did they function? What administrative philosophy, if any, guided their work? What did they accomplish and not accomplish? What is there we can learn from the earlier Hoover Commissions that is appropriate for the decade of the 1980s? Was it a unique response to a unique set of circumstances? Or, is the experience of the Hoover Commissions relevant to and replicable in our time?

The author is indebted to many people for the ideas expressed in this study. To my mentors, the late Wallace Sayre, who made me realize that political science and public administration are inseparable and Harold Seidman, who proves everyday that administrative politics is both significant and fun, I am pleased to acknowledge my debt.

I take full responsibility for whatever failings there may be in this book, but several people deserve to be thanked in print for their assistance. George Esser, President of the National Academy of Public Administration, encouraged me to publish this study and provided the funding. Reviewers James Fesler, Alan Dean, and Harold Seidman were especially generous with their time and talents. Colleagues and friends, Louis Fisher, Frederick Pauls and Robert Gilmour offered critical comments at opportune moments. My thanks go to

Eileen Gray who with care typed this manuscript. And finally, I would be remiss not to note my continuing appreciation to my wife, Grace, who provided support and solace when the going got rough.

R.C.M.

1/ U.S., Congress, Senate, Committee on Governmental Affairs, To Establish A Commission on More Effective Government, S. Rept. 179, 97th Cong., 1st sess., 1981.

2/ Carl Marcy, Presidential Commissions (New York: King's Crown Press, 1945). Frank Popper, The President's Commissions (Washington: The Twentieth Century Fund, 1970). Thomas R. Wolanin, Presidential Advisory Commissions: Truman to Nixon (Madison: University of Wisconsin Press, 1975). Terrence R. Tutchings, Rhetoric and Reality: Presidential Commissions and the Making of Public Policy (Boulder, Colorado: Westview Press, 1979).

3/ Exceptions to the generalization that most assessments of the Hoover Commissions were contemporaneous with the Commissions are to be found in two substantial, insightful, and partly critical analyses of the Commissions by political scientists. Herbert Emmerich, Federal Organization and Administrative Management (University, Alabama: University of Alabama Press, 1971), chapters 5 and 6. Harold Seidman, Politics, Position, and Power: The Dynamics of Federal Organization, 3rd ed. (New York: Oxford University Press, 1980).

4/ Peri Arnold, for instance, has written extensively both on Mr. Hoover as an administrator/theoretician and on the Commissions, relying for much of his research upon the resources of the Hoover Presidential Library. See his "The First Hoover Commission and the Managerial Presidency," Journal of Politics 38 (February 1976): 46-70.

Introduction

Over the years numerous bills have been introduced to establish
a major study commission patterned after the two Hoover Commissions
of some thirty years ago. Sponsors of these bills argue that it is
time for an overall review of the structure and functions of the
Federal Government by a group of experts that would include Members
of Congress, officers of the executive branch, representatives of
other political jurisdictions, and private sector members.

Between the years 1947 and 1955 two major studies of the organization and functions of the executive branch were undertaken.
Congress established by statute in 1947 (61 Stat. 246) a Commission
on Organization of the Executive Branch of the Government, popularly
known by the name of its chairman, former President Herbert Hoover,
as the first Hoover Commission. This Commission submitted its report with recommendations in 1949. In 1953, Congress again established (67 Stat. 184) a study commission with the same title, also
chaired by Mr. Hoover, that is referred to as the second Hoover
Commission. This Commission submitted its recommendations to the
President and to Congress in 1955. 1/

The two Hoover Commissions were not the first efforts to review
the structure and functions of the executive branch, nor were they to
be the last. What made them unusual among the studies of the executive branch, however, was that they were congressionally inspired--
although they enjoyed presidential cooperation--comprehensive in
coverage, bipartisan, and guided by a certain philosophical consensus as to the role that Government ought to play in society and the
proper role of the President in the administrative structure of the
Government. More specifically, both Commissions sought to reduce the
role of the Federal Government in the life of the Nation, reorganize
Federal agencies to produce greater "economy and efficiency" in its
operations, and generally strengthen the President and departmental
secretaries as administrative managers of the executive branch.

The First Commission was chiefly concerned with structural reorganization of departments and agencies and with upgrading the
President's managerial authorities. The second Commission dealt
more with functions performed by the executive branch and with

1

questions of policy. There was a Democratic administration, under President Harry Truman, during the period when the first Hoover Commission met and a Republican administration, under President Dwight Eisenhower, during the period when the second Hoover Commission served.

Membership on both Commissions was bipartisan. The statute establishing the first Commission required that it be composed of six Democratic and six Republican members. This requirement was absent from the enabling act of the second Commission and the partisan composition was seven members of the Republican Party and five members of the Democratic Party. Even though the Commissioners frequently filed dissents or separate views with respect to specific recommendations and in a few cases with respect to an entire report, the divisions did not occur along party lines. Every member of both Commissions filed separate views or a dissent in connection with at least one report.

There was a dualistic character to the philosophy that guided the two Hoover Commissions. The values to be promoted through reorganization were decidedly at variance between Congress on the one hand and the President and the bulk of the academic community on the other. To most members of Congress, executive reorganization was desirable if it could result in "economy and efficiency," particularly if a dollar amount of savings could be cited as a product of the reorganization. The President, and the public administration community, however, were together in the promotion of reorganization as a method to achieve "sound principles of administrative management" irrespective of whether "economies" could be reasonably expected.

To many observers, the reorganization proposals of the two Hoover Commissions, particularly the first Commission, were noteworthy because they appeared to promote greater "rationality" in the organization and operation of government agencies. A concentration on the reorganization of departments, agencies, and certain functions, while important, tends to obscure what others believed was the principal achievement of the Commissions, namely the enhancement of the presidential office as manager of the government.

In retrospect, the intellectual influence of the two Hoover Commissions appears to have lasted just over a decade. The Hoover Commissions were motivated by a distinct political and administrative philosophy. Like all philosophies, it suffered a bit when forced to accommodate to reality, but it was a fairly coherent philosophy nonetheless. There was a respect for institutional arrangement and a belief that all units performing public functions should be accountable in some manner to politically responsible officials. The administrative system should be managed by the President. The Commissions believed in hierarchical structure for the executive branch with the burden of proof for exceptions resting upon those seeking exceptions. There was also a belief that government should exercise restraint in the functions it performed. The basic strength of the political system rested, in their opinion, upon a healthy private sector.

By the mid-1960s, the philosophy that had guided the two Hoover Commissions was undergoing rapid erosion. Not only was the constituency calling for a smaller government in retreat, but the dominant academic position was clearly in favor of a larger public sector and more government involvement in all aspects of national life. 3/ Somewhat paradoxically, as more functions shifted to the public sector, the public sector became more fragmented. Increasingly, decisions were made to assign public functions to units outside the departmental structure and even, on occasion, to units outside the executive branch altogether. There was also a growing trend towards using private and government-sponsored enterprises to perform public functions. These trends profoundly altered the organization of the Federal Government and challenged the efficacy of the central managerial units of Government, including the institutionalized presidency.

While Presidents contributed to the proliferation of agencies and programs, they were also concerned that their ability to manage the Federal Establishment was declining. They sought a counterstrategy to increase their institutional leverage and looked to reorganization as a strategy to reverse the trend toward agency dispersion.

Presidents John Kennedy and Lyndon Johnson appointed many task forces to study various aspects of governmental organization and policy. 3/ Two task forces were appointed with broader mandates than the rest. The first was a Task Force on Government Reorganization chaired by Don K. Price, a Harvard University professor and veteran reorganizer. The second was a Task Force on Government Organization chaired by Ben Heineman, an industrialist. These low visibility task forces shared the fate of not having their reports made public although their indirect influence was substantial. 4/

Soon after taking office, President Richard Nixon appointed a President's Advisory Council on Executive Organization, chaired by Roy L. Ash. The Ash Council met monthly over a 14 month period and submitted some thirteen memorandums to the President. These memorandums served as the basis for the legislative proposals to reorganize much of the executive branch which the President submitted to Congress in 1971. 5/ The Ash Council study was based on a comprehensive theory of organization and management with some resemblence to the report of the first Hoover Commission. Congress rejected the President's proposals.

President Jimmy Carter came into Office bent on reorganizing the executive branch and reducing the Government from some 1900 agencies to 200. 6/ A massive President's Reorganization Project staff was assembled (estimated at 300 persons) under the loose supervision of the Office of Management and Budget. Thirty studies were begun, most were finished but none were published. The whole project, lacking a theoretical base, was generally viewed as unsuccessful. 7/

4

        Disappointments in the results of recent comprehensive reorgani-
zation efforts has in no way diminished the allure of the subject.
Presidents, Congress, professional organizations, and interest
groups, continue to call for more reorganization. The succession of
disappointments appears, ironically, to have actually enhanced the
reputation of the two Hoover Commissions as "successes" and encouraged supporters of the "citizens commission" concept to push again
for a new Hoover Commission patterned, in large measure, after the
earlier Commissions.

    1/ For a summary account of both Commissions, consult: U.S.,
Congress, House, Committee on Government Operations, Summary of the
Objectives, Operations, and Results of the Commissions on Organiza-
tion of the Executive Branch of the Government (First and Second
Hoover Commissions). Committee print, 88th Cong., 1st sess., 1963.

    2/ See, for instance, John Kenneth Galbraith, The Affluent
Society (Boston: Houghton Mifflin Company, 1958). Anthony Downs,
"Why the Government Budget Is Too Small in a Democracy," World
Politics 12 (July 1960): 541-563.

    3/ Norman C. Thomas and Harold L. Wolman, "Policy Formulation
in the Institutionalized Presidency: The Johnson Task Forces," in
The Presidential Advisory System, eds. Thomas E. Cronin and Sanford
D. Greenberg (New York: Harper and Row, 1969): 124-143.

    4/ For a detailed discussion of the work and recommendations of
both the Price and Heineman Task Forces, consult: Emmette S. Redford
and Marlin Blisett, Organizing the Executive Branch: The Johnson
Presidency (Chicago: University of Chicago Press, 1981).

    5/ President Nixon's legislative proposals to reorganize the
executive branch are found in: U.S., Executive Office of the President, Office of Management and Budget, Papers Relating to the President's Departmental Reorganization Program. Washington: U.S. Govt.
Print. Off., 1971. The Ash Council reports and the President's reorganization proposals are described and analyzed in: U.S., Congress, House, Committee on Government Operations, Executive Reorganization: A Summary Analysis, H. Rept. 922, 92d Cong., 2d sess., 1972.

    6/ U.S., Congress, Committee on Administration, The Presiden-
tial Campaign 1976: Jimmy Carter. Vol. 1, Report 1, 95th Cong., 2d
sess., 1978. pp. 581-582. The basis for the Carter assertion that
there were 1900 Federal agencies was never clear. Depending on how
the term "agency" is defined, an estimate of between 250 and 300
agencies is closer to the mark.

    7/ James Sundquist, "Jimmy Carter as Public Administrator: An
Appraisal at Mid-Term," Public Administration Review, 39 (January/
February 1979): 3-11. U.S., Library of Congress, Congressional Research Service, The Carter Reorganization Effort: A Review and Assessment, by Ronald C. Moe, Rept. No. 80-172, September 1980.

1
Philosophical Background of the Hoover Commissions

MOVEMENTS IN PUBLIC ADMINISTRATION

To understand why the two Hoover Commissions were created it is first necessary to review some administrative history. Major scholarly works are in general agreement with the view that during the early period of the discipline of public administration certain "movements" were crucial to the evolution of ideas on how the national administration ought to be organized. 1/

The overarching movement of the years from the turn of the century to the first World War was the Progressive Movement. Progressivism in politics was the successor of the earlier civil service reform efforts that had culminated, at the Federal level, in the passage of the Pendleton Act of 1883 creating the classified civil service. Having rid the political system of the worst excesses of corruption and the spoils system, the civil service reformers turned their attention to the operations of government. They sought to bring to the public sector the organizational and managerial techniques which had proven, in their opinion, so successful in the private business sector. In Progressivism, the manager had become the hero.

Closely related to the Progressive Movement was the establishment of research centers to study and promote certain public administration concepts. The first of these centers was the New York Bureau of Municipal Research which opened in 1907. 2/ This Bureau would spawn similar organizations across the Nation. "The spirit of the Bureau movement," Dwight Waldo observed, "has deeply affected public administration."

The Bureau movement was a part of Progressivism, and its leaders were leaders of Progressivism. They were tired of the simple moralism of the nineteenth century, although paradoxically they were themselves fired with moral fervor of humanitarianism and secularized Christianity. They were stirred by the revelations of the Muckrakers, but despaired of reform

5

by spontaneous combustion. They were sensitive to
the appeal and promises of science, and put a simple
trust in discovery of facts as the way of science and
as a sufficient mode for solution of human problems.
They accepted—they urged—the new positive conception
of government, and verged upon the idea of a planned
and managed society. They hated 'bad' business, but
found in business organization and procedure an acceptable prototype for public business. 3/

While reformers tended to be anti-big business, they were enamored of the corporate structure for in their minds it denoted "efficiency." The administration of business appeared to be more
"scientific" than that which characterized the public sector. What
was needed, they believed, was the application of some scientific
theory of management to the administration of public affairs.

The idea of "scientific management" is attributed to Frederick
W. Taylor who wrote on the One Best Way to manage a manufacturing
activity. 4/ Although he was specifically concerned with managing
the work process in the factory, he was convinced, as were his fol-
lowers, that the principles of Scientific Management were applicable
to public administration as well. 5/ "Taylorism" became more than
a concept for management planning, it acquired some of the trappings
of a political ideology. 6/ Many public administrators over several
generations would pin their hopes and aspirations for a better world
to Taylorism. 7/

Scientific Management was influential not so much because of its
specialized procedures as for the fundamental idea it fostered, namely, the infinite perfectability of human institutions. 8/ Properly
constructed and managed institutions, it was believed, could overcome
many of the structural inadequacies of congressionally mandated programs. There was a certain cockiness among public administrationists
that they could administer anything. Managers could and would ultimately triumph over the frailties of politicians.

Two additional movements must be credited with a role in altering the institutional character of the executive branch. First, soon
after the turn of the century, there appeared writings supporting the
concept of an executive budget. And second, there was a belief that
"economy and efficiency" could be achieved if the Federal Government
was reorganized to increase presidential and secretarial authority.

In the years preceding this century, the President had relatively little control over either the national budget or over the administration of the laws. While Presidents and Secretaries of the
Treasury were not passive bystanders in the budgetary process prior
to the passage of the Budget and Account Act of 1921, they were most
often cast in the role of the "protector of the purse." 9/ Presidents were not responsible for planning and implementing the budget,
rather they were expected to use their veto power as a "watchdog" to
prevent outrageous proposals and scandalous expenditures.

One element of Progressivism was the movement to institute a national budget. 10/ The shift of budget responsibilities from the legislative body to the executive was first accomplished in several instances at the local and State level. Several years of budget deficits persuaded Congress in 1909 to direct the Secretary of the Treasury to estimate revenues for the next year and to make recommendations for new taxes if there were anticipated deficiencies. 11/ The Secretary of the Treasury and President William Howard Taft attempted to meet the congressional request but found the experience frustrating as the necessary information was not readily available. President Taft requested, and Congress appropriated, funds to study the financial management of the executive agencies. A five member Commission on Economy and Efficiency met for over two years and in June 1912, President Taft forwarded a proposal to Congress to establish a national budget with the President being responsible for reviewing departmental estimates and submitting a single document. 12/ This proposal languished for nine years finally reaching fruition with the passage of the Budget and Accounting Act of 1921 (42 Stat. 20).

Reorganization of executive agencies and functions as a systematic tool of governance was another movement to be credited to Progressivism. "President Theodore Roosevelt, unlike McKinley," Herbert Emmerich averred, "had firm views on presidential management. He was the undoubted originator of the concept of reorganization as a continuing need of administrative management and as an executive responsibility." 13/ Roosevelt, the embodiment of Progressivism, believed that a corollary of Scientific Management was the view that there was a best way to organize the executive branch and that the prerogative to reorganize should rest with the President and his departmental secretaries. The 1903 Act creating the Department of Commerce and Labor (32 Stat. 827) authorized the President " . . . by order in writing, to transfer to the new department any unit engaged in statistical or scientific work, together with their duties and authority." The authority for a transfer would then be an Executive order rather than a statute. Roosevelt subsequently asked Congress, unsuccessfully, for broad reorganization authority. 14/ Later Presidents would press with greater success for general reorganization powers.

World War I brought to a close the Progressive Era, but the several administrative movements which had been an integral part of Progressivism's philosophy remained to influence following generations and continue, in many respects, to exert an influence over administrative thought today.

STUDIES OF GOVERNMENT ORGANIZATION

The two Hoover Commissions were not the first attempts to study the organization of the executive branch. They followed in the steps of previous efforts and benefitted from what had gone before.

On the other hand, they were also constrained to a certain degree
by these prior studies if for no other reason than the fact that
they felt obligated to differ somewhat in their recommendations
from, say, the Brownlow Committee Report of 1937.

There had been a number of studies of the executive branch completed prior to World War II. What follows is a brief description
of these studies, several of which have subsequently attained the
status of landmarks in Federal administrative development. Both the
President and Congress exhibited initiative in the field of executive
reorganization. These studies, reflecting the dominant administrative theories of the moment, did result in many structural, proce-
dural, and programmatic reorganizations in the decades prior to the
creation of the Hoover Commissions.

Congressional Commissions

Although there had been official inquiries into events and activities since the inception of the Republic, Congress greatly
expanded its investigatory activity during the final third of the
19th century. 15/ The two most comprehensive inquiries were a select
committee of the Senate (Cockrell Committee) which functioned between
1887 and 1889 16/ and a joint commission (Dockery-Cockrell Commission) which met between 1893 and 1895.

The principal significance of these two commissions for administrative history lies not in their substantive results, which were
minimal, but rather in their attitudes towards the institutional
Presidency and its relationship to the departments and agencies.
Neither inquiry discussed the Presidential office nor what role that
office might be expected to play in the improvement of the conduct of
the executive branch. 18/

With the onset of the new century, various factors combined to
thrust the President into a more active and supervisorial role with
respect to the administrative agencies. America had just fought a
successful war and had become an international power. The President's constitutional responsibilities with regard to foreign affairs
and the conduct of defense matters was more direct than it was with
purely domestic matters. As governmental intervention in the economy
became more prevalent, Congress found it increasingly difficult to
direct Federal activities by legislation and chose, instead, to delegate authority to the President and agency heads. The effect of such
delegation was to increase the degree of administrative supervision
exercised by the President.

Keep Commission

The first overall effort to review the workings of the executive
agencies from a presidential perspective was undertaken by the Commission on Department Methods (1905-1909), otherwise known as the
Keep Commission, after its chairman, Charles Hallam Keep, Assistant
Secretary of the Treasury. Although the Commission did not publish
a complete report on its activites, a number of its studies did find
their way into congressional documents. The findings of the Commission stimulated management improvements in many bureaus and in
such fields as accounting and costing, archives and records management, simplification of paperwork, and improvements in personnel
administration, procurement, supply, and contracting procedures. 19/

Committee on Economy and Efficiency

President William Howard Taft appointed a Committee on Economy
and Efficiency in 1910 which worked through the remainder of his
Administration. During this period the Committee, under the leadership of Frederick A. Cleveland, then Director of the Bureau of
Municipal Research of New York City, issued a number of extensive
reports including the first detailed account of how the executive
branch was organized for the performance of its work and a report,
as discussed previously, advocating a "national budget" and the
establishment of a Bureau of the Budget. 20/

Joint Committee on Reorganization

In the early 1920s, there was a concerted effort by the Congress
and the President to study the organization of the executive branch
and to propose recommendations for change. 21/ Most notable in this
regard was the establishment of the Joint Committee on the Reorganization of the Administrative Branch of the Government. Congress
created in December 1920, a joint committee of three members of the
Senate and three members of the House. 22/ By joint resolution in
May 1921, the President was authorized to appoint a representative
"to cooperate" with the Committee. 23/ President Harding appointed
one of his secretaries, Walter F. Brown, who was subsequently selected as chairman of the Joint Committee by its members.

The Joint Committee did not conduct an independent study of or-
ganization of the executive branch. Instead, it relied on the
President, who submitted his ideas in the form of an address to a
Joint Session of Congress. Although Congress had for all intents

and purposes turned the initiative over to the President, the Chief
Executive did not have the institutional resources to conduct a
major study of his own. He, therefore, had to rely on Walter Brown
and whatever support he might find from the Cabinet. And in this
regard the President was most fortunate to have a Secretary of Commerce whose judgment he trusted.

   The major intellectual thrust in this reorganization
   effort came not from the President or Brown, but from the
   Secretary of Commerce, Herbert Hoover. Hoover was vitally
   interested in reorganization, and to this day stands out
   as perhaps the most prominent theoretician-practitioner in
   American public administration. Beyond this, Hoover was
   the pillar of the Harding Cabinet. The President trusted
   his Secretary of Commerce and tended to rely on Hoover
   for advice on a wide range of policy matters. While
   President Harding used his position to support the reorganization planning effort, and Walter Brown offered the
   legitimizing aegis of the Joint Committee and served as
   coordinator, Herbert Hoover provided the intellectual
   thrust for the endeavor. 24/

After much jurisdictional strife within the Cabinet over what
organizational recommendations ought to be included in the President's report, 25/ the report was forwarded to the Joint Committee
in June 1923. The Committee held hearings 26/ and then made its
report to Congress. 27/ In its report, the Joint Committee largely adopted the President's recommendations. The leaders of Congress were not persuaded, however, by the Joint Committee's report
and no action was forthcoming. The experience of the Joint Committee, while not productive of organizational change, was important in that it tended to galvanize support for the concept of
the President as manager of the executive branch, and in this
sense served as a precursor of the Brownlow Committee in 1936. 28/

This initial foray into executive reorganization did highlight
the divergence in values between Congress on the one hand and the
President and the bulk of the academic community on the other. To
Congress, executive branch reorganization was desirable if it could
result in "economy," particularly if the economies could be measured
in dollar figures. The President, and the emerging discipline of
public administration, however, tended to see in executive reorganization a means to achieve "sound principles of administrative management" irrespective of whether "economies" could be reasonably expected. Herbert Hoover was unusual in that he wanted to reorganize
the executive branch to maximize both value systems.

Brownlow Committee

The Democratic Platform of 1932 promised "an immediate and drastic reduction of governmental expenditures by abolishing useless commissions and offices, consolidating departments and bureaus, and eliminating extravagance, to accomplish a saving of not less than twenty-five percent in (the) cost of (the) Federal government . . . ." 29/ Soon after taking office, however, Franklin Roosevelt decided that the exigencies of the moment militated against a comprehensive reorganization and instead he opted for minor changes in structure and for the creation of many new agencies and government corporations to perform tasks not previously assigned to the Federal Government. Most of the new agencies and government corporations were located outside the regular executive departments.

Senator Harry F. Byrd, Sr., concerned that reorganization was resulting in more, rather than less, government spending, successfully persuaded the Senate in February 1936, to create a special committee to investigate the executive branch. The Committee subsequently let a contract with the Brookings Institution to prepare a report. 30/ The President, partly in response to the congressional initiative, appointed his own President's Committee on Administrative Management consisting of Louis Brownlow as Chairman, and Charles Merriam and Luther Gulick as members. This three member panel assured the President that their final product would be to his liking. 31/

There was considerable conflict between the supporters of the Brookings Institution study and those supporting the President's Committee, known thereafter after its chairman, Louis Brownlow. The results of the 1936 election, however, tipped the scales in favor of the President. He wanted a "report on principles, not details." 32/ A research staff of 26 persons was assembled, composed largely of political scientists and public administrators. The staff papers and memoranda tended to be conceptually oriented with the Committee writing a relatively short, general report to the President.

The Report of the Brownlow Committee was submitted to Congress in January 1937. 33/ The principal thesis of the report was that the executive branch ought to be reorganized to create an integrated, hierarchical structure with the President as an active manager. A strong argument was forthcoming on the virtues of "departmentalism." The report proposed, among other things, that some 100 independent agencies, administrations, boards and commissions be placed within 12 executive departments. Of these departments, two—Public Works and Social Welfare—would be new additions to the Cabinet. The report was particularly harsh on the independent regulatory commissions, referring to them as the "headless fourth branch of government."

12

       The independent commissions present a serious im-
mediate problem. No administrative reorganization worthy
of the name can leave hanging in the air more than a
dozen powerful, irresponsible agencies free to determine
policy and administer law. Any program to restore our
constitutional ideal of a fully coordinated Executive
Branch responsible to the President must bring within
the reach of that responsible control all work done by
these independent commissions which is not judicial in
nature. That challenge cannot be ignored. 34/

       The President submitted an Executive Reorganization bill in 1938
which contained many of the specific recommendations of the Brownlow
Committee, but it was defeated in Congress, in part over concern that
it would give too much power to the President and abet what many saw
that year as a trend towards "Presidential dictatorship." 35/

       In February 1939, still smarting from the defeat suffered the
previous year, the President sent forward another Reorganization Act.
This bill, however, was noteworthy for its apparent modest scope. It
contained only two of the major proposals recommended by the Brownlow
Committee. The bill authorized the President to appoint six administrative assistants and to submit reorganization plans to alter
executive branch organization, such plans being subject to a veto by
a concurrent resolution. 36/ While there was considerable concern
expressed regarding the constitutionality of the procedures outlined
for approving reorganization plans, the House and Senate passed the
bill (53 Stat. 651). 37/

       In terms of legislative accomplishments, relatively little was
forthcoming from the Brownlow Committee's work. The two most important results were the passage of the Reorganization Act of 1939 and
the establishment, by way of Reorganization Plan No. 1 of 1939, of
the Executive Office of the President. The Committee's greatest
legacy, 38/ however, lay in the refinement of the concept of Presidential management, much of which would find fruition in the accepted
recommendations of the two Hoover Commissions.

HERBERT HOOVER AS ADMINISTRATOR AND REORGANIZER

       The two Hoover Commissions cannot be understood without first
recognizing the crucial role played in their deliberations and recommendations by their chairman, former President Herbert Hoover. It
may not be much of an overstatement to suggest that the two Commissions were largely an extension of the personality and beliefs of
Mr. Hoover.

In recent years there has been a major shift in scholarly opinion regarding the administrative philosophy and accomplishments of Hoover, first as Secretary of Commerce and later as President. 39/ For the most part, this re-evaluation of Hoover has been sympathetic and has constituted a rejection of the heretofore dominant academic viewpoint. The prevailing intellectual framework, until recently, was established by historians supportive of the New Deal. 40/ To them, Hoover represented an outmoded approach to Government and they cavalierly dismissed attempts to study Hoover's philosophy, policies, and activities in a serious manner.

The reigning assumptions of this framework continued to hold that modern America had taken shape during its reform presidencies, especially those of Theodore Roosevelt, Woodrow Wilson, and Franklin D. Roosevelt. The periods between them had been barren, frivolous, or reactionary interludes, deserving and receiving little historical study. And in the absence of such study, the anti-Hoover rhetoric of 1932 and 1933 continued to be accepted as historical reality. 41/

The emergence of "revisionist" literature on Hoover 42/ is in substantial measure traceable to the opening of the Hoover Library at West Branch, Iowa, in 1966. The establishment of the Library, with its wealth of primary data, coincided in time with the development of new frameworks for historical analysis which generally rejected the view that American history could be explained in terms of the predominant influence of the "reformist" Presidents or that the years between the first World War and the Depression were barren and irrelevant. 43/

The revisionists may differ in their approaches but they generally conclude that Hoover was a "modern" President, not the last of the "old" Presidents, and that his administrative leadership in the Department of Commerce and as President reflected the continuity of public policy rather than the end of a political order. 44/

Hoover's concept of governmental administration, as Secretary of Commerce, as President, and later as Chairman of the Commissions, was strongly influenced by Progressivism and the tenets of Scientific Management. He believed in fact-finding, research, and planning, and, like the first Roosevelt, 45/ he was enamored of "blue ribbon" study commissions. 46/ His experience, first as an international business executive, then as administrator of a massive food distribution system under wartime and revolutionary conditions, gave him two tools indispensable to his later political career. He acquired a cadre of devoted younger colleagues as well as a comprehensive philosophy of adminstration that stressed the necessity of strong leadership emanating from a single executive. 47/ Hoover became the quintessence of the new, twentieth-century man, the public manager.

In 1921, a newly elected President Warren Harding, after considerable political manuevering, was able to appoint Hoover as his
Secretary of Commerce. Buoyed by his wartime experience, Hoover
brought to his new job a fairly comprehensive political and administrative philosophy. For Hoover, individual opportunity and security
were the benchmarks by which to measure the good society, not the
enlargement of the state. Individual opportunity and success in the
new, postwar society, according to Hoover, depended upon voluntary
cooperation between the individual and private organizations, and the
government. Hoover appeared to be more interested in bringing stability to the business community than in promoting competition. 48/

The secret to attaining economic stability, in Hoover's view,
was the creation of trade associations which would provide a clear-
inghouse for industry information and a framework for "cooperative
effort." In turn, the government would work closely with these trade
associations. Hoover's philosophy has been described by the term
"associative state." 49/ He wanted planned progress, but with the
planners not being the corps of political executives and their com
patriots, the permanent civil service. Hoover was a bureaucratic in-
novator seeking to create structures to manage our growing society
without relying on burdensome state organizations and procedures. 50/

As Secretary of Commerce, Hoover set out to reorganize much of
the executive branch. His immediate objective was to alter and expand the functions of the Department of Commerce. During the course
of discussions in 1921 within the executive branch, he proposed three
great divisions for the Department, one for industry, one for trade,
and one for transportation and commerce. A variety of agencies would
then be shifted to the Commerce Department. Ellis Hawley observed of
Hoover's early reorganization effort:

> In essence, the commerce department was to become
> a department of economic development and management; other
> agencies would still be responsible for special sectors
> of the economy, but commerce would serve as a general
> policy coordinator . . . .
> Reaching out from this expanded governmental base
> would be an extensive net of promotional activities,
> cooperating commissions, and other ad hoc structures,
> all tied to private groupings and associations and
> all designed to energize private and local collectiv-
> ities and guide them toward constructive solutions to
> national problems. 51/

The Department of Commerce was to be the foundation of the Associative State. Opposition within the Cabinet to Hoover's proposal
was immediate and intense. 52/ Although their reasons varied, the
several departments and the bureaus within the departments fought
vigorously against the "scientific" proposals of the Commerce Secretary. As a result, the Administration was slow in submitting a
comprehensive reorganization proposal to Congress, was less than
vigorous in its support, and Congress decided not to act.

Speaking before the Joint Committee on Reorganization in 1924, Hoover recommended that Congress give the authority, within specified limits, to the President to reorganize executive departments and agencies. 53/ Hoover continued to speak on this theme over the next few years. In 1925, Hoover summarized the views that would remain his philosophy through the next three decades, including the period of the two Hoover Commissions. "For the most part they [agencies] have been thrown hodge-podge into the different executive departments under Cabinet officers. But there are more than forty independent establishments," Hoover lamented, "either directly under the President or directly under Congress." He then went on to elaborate on the consequences of this proliferation in governmental organizations.

> As this immense number of bureaus and agencies
> is now grouped and organized there are six primary
> streams of confusion and waste. There is a confusion
> of basic principles; there is a grouping of Federal
> bureaus which divides responsibility; there arises
> from this scattering a lack of definite national
> policies; direct waste arises from overlap and
> conflict; indirectly large costs are imposed upon
> citizens by this scattering of functions and by the
> undue complexity of laws and regulations. There
> are too many floating islands in this dismal swamp
> of independent agencies only technically anchored
> to the President but really responsible to nobody—
> and with all this division of authority multiplies
> the urge for expansion of Federal activities in
> every direction. 59/

In his 1929 Annual Message to Congress the now President Hoover requested authority to reorganize the executive branch, subject to some form of congressional disapproval. 55/ Over the next three years, Hoover would often return to this subject. As the 1932 election approached, both parties called for reductions in Government spending and reorganization was perceived as one method to achieve this objective. In June 1932, Congress voted the President authority to reorganize the executive branch by Executive order, subject to a one-House veto. 56/ Shortly thereafter, Congress adjourned. When Congress reconvened in December 1932, President Hoover issued eleven Executive orders consolidating some 58 governmental activities. 57/ By that time, however, Hoover had been overwhelmingly defeated in the general election. Congress was in no mood to give the lame-duck President its approval and by a voice vote passed the resolution of disapproval disallowing all eleven Executive orders. 58/

Although to Herbert Hoover "belongs the undoubted credit for the invention and espousal of the important peacetime reorganization device—presidential initiative subject to the legislative veto," 59/ it remained to his successor, Franklin Roosevelt, to be the first President to use this authority successfully. With Hoover's defeat, he passed from the limelight although his interest in Government organization remained undimmed.

1/ Dwight Waldo, The Administrative State: A Study in the Political Theory of American Public Administration (New York: Ronald Press, 1948), pp. 22-47. Leonard D. White, Trends in Public Administration (New York: McGraw-Hill Book Company, 1933), chapter 22.

2/ Gustavus A. Weber, Organized Efforts for the Improvement of Methods of Administration in the United States (New York: D. Appleton and Company, 1919), chapter 6.

3/ Waldo, The Administrative State, p. 32.

4/ Frederick W. Taylor, The Principles of Scientific Management (New York: Harper and Bros., 1911).

5/ Testimony of Frederick W. Taylor before Special Committee of the House of Representatives to Investigate the Taylor and Other Systems of Shop Management, Jan. 25, 1912. The Committee reported its findings to the House on Mar. 9, 1912. (62d Cong., 2d sess., H. Rept. 403).

6/ Dwight Waldo commented on Taylorism: "Scientific Management is a system almost as elaborate as Marxism with its central figures, its schisms, its mutations, its nuances, etc." The Administrative State, p. 47.

7/ "Our administrators of the future," John Pfiffner declared in 1940, "must be good managers. They must know the techniques of scientific management. Indeed, it may well be that the principles of Frederick W. Taylor, adopted to social ends, will some day free the world of drudgery, and it will be remembered that fact-finding and research is a fundamental of Taylorism. What is needed is the development of a school of management research technicians who possess the just, wise, and omniscient qualities of Plato's guardians." Research Methods in Public Administration (New York, Ronald Press, 1940), p. 25.

8/ Leonard D. White, Introduction to the Study of Public Administration, 4th ed. (New York: Macmillan Company, 1955), p. 21.

9/ Louis Fisher, Presidential Spending Power (Princeton, Princeton University Press, 1975), pp. 9-27.

10/ W. F. Willoughby, The Problem of a National Budget (New York, D. Appleton Co., 1918).

11/ Fisher, Presidential Spending Power, pp. 27-55.

12/ U.S. President's Committee on Economy and Efficiency. The Need for National Budget. Submitted in the form of a Message from the President to Congress. House Doc. 854. 62d Cong., 2d sess., June 27, 1912.

13/ Herbert Emmerich, Federal Organization and Administrative Management (University, Alabama, University of Alabama Press, 1971), p. 38.

14/ James D. Richardson, ed., Seventh Annual Message of President Theodore Roosevelt to Congress. Messages and Papers of the President, v. XIV (New York: Bureau of National Literature, 1918), p. 7105.

15/ For a bibliography of congressional inquiries into the conduct of business of the executive departments other than by standing committee, 1789-1911, consult: Gustavus Weber, Organized Efforts for the Improvement of Methods of Administration (New York: D. Appleton and Company, 1919), pp. 45-56.

16/ Oscar Kraines, "The Cockrell Committee, 1887-1889: First Comprehensive Congressional Investigation into Administration," Western Political Quarterly 4 (December 1951): 583-609.

17/ Weber, Organized Efforts for the Improvement of Methods of Administration in the United States, pp. 66-73.

18/ Oscar Kraines observed of the early congressional efforts: "Established and motivated by legislative action, the Cockrell Committee, like the inquiries preceding it and the Dockery-Cockrell Commission which followed it, assumed accountability of administration to the legislature. Accordingly, the Committee paid no attention and did not consider the concept of accountability of administration to the executive." "The Cockrell Committee, 1887-1889," p. 607.

19/ Oscar Kraines, "The President Versus Congress: The Keep Commission, 1905-1909, First Comprehensive Presidential Inquiry in Administration," Western Political Quarterly 23 (March 1970): 5-54.

20/ For a discussion of the work and publications of the Committee on Economy and Efficiency, see: Weber, Organized Efforts for the Improvement of Methods of Administration, pp. 84-103.

21/ For a summary account of reorganization studies completed in the 1920s, consult: Edward H. Hobbs, Executive Reorganization in the National Government (University, Mississippi: University of Mississippi Press, 1953), pp. 21-34.

22/ Joint Resolution of December 29, 1920 (41 Stat. 1083).

23/ Joint Resolution of May 5, 1921 (41 Stat. 4). This Joint
Resolution provides one of the most unusual examples of legislative-
executive cooperation to be found in the statute books as it autho-
rizes the President to appoint a "Representative of the Executive
to cooperate with the Joint Committee on Reorganization . . . who
shall receive an annual salary of $7,500, payable monthly, such
salary to be paid in equal parts from contingent funds of the
Senate and House."

24/ Peri Arnold, "Executive Reorganization and Administrative
Theory: The Origins of the Managerial Presidency." Paper delivered
at the 1976 Annual Meeting of the American Political Science Association. p. 12.

25/ Edward L. and Frederick H. Schapsmeier, "Disharmony in the
Harding Cabinet," Ohio History 75 (Spring/Summer 1966): 126-136, 188-
190.

26/ U.S., Joint Committee on Reorganization of the Administrative Branch of the Government, Reorganization of Executive Departments, Hearings on S.J.Res. 282, 68th Cong., 1st sess., 1924.

27/ Congressional Record, v. 65, June 3, 1924. p. 10252.

28/ The view that the Joint Committee was a worthy precursor of
the Brownlow Committee is ably argued by Peri Arnold in his paper
delivered at the 1976 Annual Meeting of the American Political
Science Association, cited above.

29/ Donald Bruce Johnson, comp., National Party Platforms:
1840-1956, rev. ed. (Urbana: University of Illinois Press, 1978),
p. 331.

30/ U.S., Congress, Senate, Select Committee to Investigate the
Executive Agencies of the Government, Investigation of Executive
Agencies of the Government (Preliminary Report) S. Rept. 1289, 75th
Cong., 1st sess., 1937. A subsidiary product of the Brookings
Institution study was: Lewis Meriam and Laurence F. Schmeckebier.
Reorganization of the National Government: What Does It Involve?
(Washington: The Brookings Institution, 1939).

31/ Richard Polenberg, Reorganizing Roosevelt's Government:
The Controversy Over Executive Reorganization, (Cambridge: Harvard
University Press, 1966), p. 7.

32/ Emmerich, Federal Organization and Administrative Management, p. 50.

33/ U.S., President's Committee on Administrative Management,
Report With Special Studies (Washington, U.S. Govt. Print. Off.,
1937).

34/ Ibid., p. 37.

35/ For an excellent account of New Deal reorganization efforts generally, and of the Executive Reorganization Bill of 1938 in particular, consult: Polenberg, Reorganizing Roosevelt's Government. Also: Barry Dean Karl, Executive Reorganization and Reform in the New Deal: The Genesis of Administrative Management, 1900-1939 (Cambridge: Harvard University Press, 1963).

36/ John D. Millett and Lindsay Rogers. "The Legislative Veto and the Reorganization Act of 1939," Public Administration Review 1 (Winter 1941): 176-189.

37/ For an extended discussion of the constitutional debate surrounding the passage of the 1939 Reorganization Act, and subsequent Reorganization Acts, consult: Louis Fisher and Ronald C. Moe, "Delegating With Ambivalence: The Legislative Veto and Reorganization Authority," IN U.S., Congress, House, Committee on Rules, Studies on the Legislative Veto, Committee print, 96th Cong., 2d sess., 1980, pp. 164-247.

38/ Harvey Mansfield, "Federal Executive Reorganization: Thirty Years of Experience," Public Administration Review 29 (July/August 1969): 332-345.

39/ A recent series of essays has attempted to explore the various elements of the public life of Mr. Hoover in light of currently available records. U.S., Congress, Senate, Herbert Hoover Reassessed: Essays Commemorating the Fiftieth Anniversary of the Inauguration of Our Thirty-First President, Senate Doc. 63, 96th Cong., 2d sess., 1981.

40/ Illustrative of the literature that relegates Herbert Hoover to the backwaters of American political and administrative history are: Arthur Schlesinger, Jr., Crisis of the Older Order, 1919-1933 (Boston: Houghton-Mifflin, 1957). Richard Hofstadter, The American Political Tradition and the Men Who Made It (New York: A. A. Knopf, 1948).

41/ Ellis W. Hawley, "Herbert Hoover and Modern American History: Fifty Years After," Congressional Record, (Daily edition), February 27, 1980, p. S1928.

42/ Representative entries in the list of revisionary works on Herbert Hoover would include: David Burner, Hoover Hoover: A Public Life (New York: A. A. Knopf, 1979). Carl Degler, "The Ordeal of Herbert Hoover," Yale Review 52 (Summer 1963): 563-583. Jordan Schwarz, The Interregnum of Despair: Hoover, Congress and the Depression (Urbana: University of Illinois Press, 1972). William Appleman Williams, The Contours of American History (Cleveland: World Publishing Company, 1961).

43/ Burl Noggle, "The Twenties: A New Historiographical Frontier," Journal of American History 53 (September 1966): 299-314.

20

44/ Peri Arnold, "Herbert Hoover and the Continuity of Public Policy," Public Policy 20 (Fall 1972), p. 526.

45/ "Theodore Roosevelt probably most deserves the title of 'Father of the Presidential Advisory Commission.' In implementing his stewardship theory of the presidency, he was first to employ groups of nongovernment experts to examine problems of public policy." Thomas R. Wolanin, Presidential Advisory Commissions: Truman to Nixon (Madison: University of Wisconsin Press, 1975), p. 5.

46/ Proof of Hoover's commitment to social science research is to be found in one of the most extraordinary, and largely ignored, research projects in American history. As President, Hoover promoted a three year project, the President's Research Committee on Social Trends, to study all major aspects of American society; e.g., "Political, Economic, and Social Activities of Women," "The Growth of the Federal Government, 1915-1932," with the objective being to "supply the basis for the formulation of large national polities looking to the next phase of the nation's development." The products of this effort were two stout volumes and thirteen substantial monographs. Recent Social Trends in the United States: Report of the President's Research Committee on Social Trends, 2v, (New York: McGraw-Hill Book Company, 1933) See; Arthur N. Holcombe, "Report on Recent Social Trends in the United States," American Political Science Review 27 (April 1933): 222-227.

47/ Herbert Hoover, The Memoirs of Herbert Hoover: Years of Adventure, 1874-1920 (New York: Macmillan Company, 1951), pp. 241-242. Hoover gives himself credit for suggesting the term "administrator" to Woodrow Wilson so that the latter could have a "neutral" word to apply to individuals selected to run programs. Prior to this time, Wilson had tried to manage the war effort through committees, in large part out of fear that if he appointed one person to manage a program, the press would label that person "czar."

48/ Herbert Hoover, "We Can Cooperate and Yet Compete," Nation's Business 14 (June 15, 1926): 11-14.

49/ Ellis W. Hawley, "Herbert Hoover, the Commerce Secretariat, and the Vision of the 'Associative State,' 1921-1928," The Journal of American History 61 (June 1974): 116-140.

50/ In describing Herbert Hoover as an administrator, Peri Arnold states: "He was a remarkably talented, modern administrator who understood the breadth of possibilities present in expansive public bureaucracy . . . . His disagreement with the New Deal's use of the state was a disagreement over policy and not an attack on modern state bureaucracy itself, which Hoover had used brilliantly during the 1920s." "The 'Great Engineer' as Administrator: Herbert Hoover and Modern Bureaucracy," Review of Politics 42 (July 1980), p. 347.

51/ Hawley, "Herbert Hoover, the Commerce Secretariat, and the vision of the 'Associative State,' 1921-1928," p. 121.

52/ Edward L. and Frederick H. Schapsmeier, "Disharmony in the Harding Cabinet," Ohio History 75 (Spring/Summer 1966), p. 135.

53/ U.S, Congress, Joint Committee on the Reorganization of Executive Departments, Reorganization of the Executive Departments, Hearings, 68th Cong., 1s sess., 1924. p. 353.

54/ Ray Lyman Wilbur and Arthur Mastick Hyde, The Hoover Policies, (New York: Charles Scribner's Sons, 1937), pp. 561-562.

55/ U.S., Public Papers of the Presidents: Herbert Hoover (1929) (Washington: U.S. Govt. Print. Off., 1974), p. 432.

56/ 47 Stat. 413. The reorganization authority was contained in Part II of the Legislative Appropriations Act for Fiscal Year 1933, popularly known as the Economy Act of 1932.

57/ Congressional Record, v. 76, December 9, 1932. pp. 233-254.

58/ Congressional Record, v. 76, January 19, 1933. pp. 2125-2126.

59/ Emmerich, Federal Organization and Administrative Management, p. 43.

2
The First Hoover Commission

LEGISLATIVE BACKGROUND

The end of the Roosevelt tenure as President and the close of World War II came within months during the year 1945. The new President, Harry S. Truman, assumed the office with the definite opinion that his predecessor had not been a particular good manager. 1/ Truman's first concern was to achieve an orderly reconversion of the economy from a war to a peacetime basis. He believed, at least initially, that substantial reorganization would be necessary.

The President requested, and Congress approved, the Reorganization Act of 1945 (59 Stat. 613) which authorized the President to submit reorganization plans subject to fewer restrictions than had been present in the 1939 Reorganization Act. Under this Act, Congress had to pass a concurrent resolution of disapproval in order to negate a presidentially submitted plan. 2/ The President believed that reorganization was peculiarly a presidential responsibility of a continuing nature. Under the 1945 Act, the President submitted six reorganization plans, four of which became effective. This appeared to some a piecemeal approach, however, not likely to result in the "reforms" deemed urgently necessary.

Throughout 1946, Republican Congressman Clarence Brown studied previous efforts to reorganize the executive branch. Incremental proposals had yielded, in his opinion, disappointing results and he concluded that what was needed was a "blue ribbon" commission to review the entire Government and to make recommendations for reorganization. 3/ The opportunity to realize his objective followed the 1946 congressional elections when a Republican majority displaced the Democratic majority in both the House and Senate. Brown introduced a bill in the House to establish a "mixed commission" consisting of Members of Congress, appointees from the executive branch, and representatives from the private sector, to study the organization of the executive branch and to submit recommendations to both the President and Congress. Senator Henry Cabot Lodge introduced an identical bill in the Senate.

The bills were referred to the Committees on Expenditures in
the Executive Departments of the respective chambers and both Committees held hearings and voted unanimously to favorably report
the bills. On June 26, 1947, the House considered the bill briefly
and passed it by voice vote without dissent. 4/ On the day following, the Senate acted on the House bill and voted its approval unanimously. 5/ As Ferrel Heady observed: "The proposal had a singu-
larly easy journey through the legislative mill. No alteration of
the language of the bill as originally introduced occurred at any
stage; nor was a single vote recorded against the proposal, either
in committee or on the floor." 6/ This bill had achieved the
"motherhood" status that exempts proposed legislation from serious
questions or opposition.

The Declaration of Policy in the Act's preamble constituted a
restatement of the "orthodox philosophy" of public administration
with its emphasis on "economy and efficiency." 7/ The nonpartisan
character of the Declaration of Policy notwithstanding, there was
concern expressed at the time that the Commission was really a
partisan wolf in sheep's clothing. With the approach of the 1948
presidential election, certain Democrats feared that the Commission
might come forth with a blueprint for dismantling the results of the
New Deal. Their anxiety was not without foundation. As Frank
Gervasi, a sympathetic observer of the first Hoover Commission commented:

> There is no doubt that the Commission's ultimate
> plan was to have been keyed to a Republican Administration
> which everyone, except Truman and some 23,000,000 Ameri-
> cans who voted for him, anticipated in November, 1948.
> The Commission's findings and recommendations for changes
> in executive organizational structure were to have been
> the grand overture of a new Republican era. 8/

In point of fact, there were deliberate efforts to keep the
Commission as nonpartisan as possible. 9/ Even the timing of the
report was designed to minimize the incentive for partisan manipu-
lation of the Commission. "In light of the temper of the times,"
Herbert Emmerich would subsequently comment, "the restraint exercised by the Congress in passing the law which authorized the
establishment of the first Hoover Commission . . . was astonish-
ing." 10/

Within ten days after the convening of the 81st Congress (January 1949), the Commission was required to submit its report and
recommendations to Congress. 11/ Within 90 days after submitting
the report, the Commission would be disbanded.

THE COMMISSION

The Commission consisted of twelve members: four appointed by the President, two from the executive branch and two from private life; four appointed by the President pro tempore of the Senate, two from the Senate and two from private life; and four appointed by the Speaker of the House of Representatives, two from the House and two from private life. Of each class of two members, one had to be from each of the "two major political parties." The Commission was to elect its own chairman and vice chairman.

In order to accomplish the purposes set forth in the legislation, the Commission was empowered to hold hearings, administer oaths of witnesses, and every executive agency was directed to furnish such information, suggestions, estimates, and statistics as might be properly requested by the chairman and vice chairman. Compensation for members was stipulated in the Act. 12/

The Commission was given the power to appoint and fix compensation of such personnel as it deemed advisable, in accordance with the provisions of the civil service laws. An initial appropriations of $750,000 was voted. 13/

Membership

The three appointing officers lost little time in announcing their choices. Republican Arthur Vandenburg, President pro tempore of the Senate, appointed Senators George Aiken (R-Vt) and John L. McClellan (D-Ark), chairman and ranking minority member of the Committee on Expenditures in the Executive Departments, the committee with jurisdiction over reorganization matters. Vandenburg's two appointees from the private sector were James K. Pollock, a professor of political science at the University of Michigan, a Republican, and Joseph P. Kennedy, formerly chairman of the Securities and Exchange Commission and Ambassador to Great Britain, a Democrat.

Speaker of the House, Joseph Martin, named as representatives of the House, Congressman Clarence Brown, Republican, and Carter Manasco, 15/ Democrat. Both gentlemen were senior members of the House Committee on Expenditures in the Executive Departments. From the private sector, Martin named former President Herbert Hoover and James Rowe, Democrat, the latter known principally for his service in staff positions under President Franklin Roosevelt.

President Truman announced his appointments on July 17, 1947. His Democratic appointee from within the executive branch was James A. Forrestal, head of what was then called the National Military Establishment. 16/ For his Republican member, Truman selected Arthur Flemming, a member of the Civil Service Commission. From

private life, Truman chose Republican George Mead, the owner and
chief executive officer of the Mead Corporation, a large paper and
pulp manufacturing corporation in Ohio. Dean Acheson was Truman's
Democratic choice from private life. Acheson had served in both
the Treasury and State Departments and was then in private law
practice.

The twelve men appointed brought their personal prestige to
the Commission. They were not selected because they constituted
a "representative" sampling of the populace or of interest groups,
rather they were chosen because of institutional positions they
occupied or special experience in Government they were believed
to possess. There was general optimism expressed by the media,
at the outset, that the Commission would prove equal to the task
at hand. 17/

Mandate

Considerable publicity attended the establishment of the Hoover
Commission. Within the Commission, however, there were divergent attitudes evident immediately that threatened the success of the venture. There were clashes over interpretations of the intent of the
enabling legislation. The congressional grant of authority covered
the entire executive branch, yet it was vague regarding what direction the Commission was expected to follow and the type of product
to be submitted to Congress.

According to the statute, the Commission might recommend reducing Government expenditures "to the lowest amount consistent with
the efficient performance of essential services," and was authorized
to recommend "abolishing services, activities, and functions not
necessary to the efficient conduct of government." To those who
interpreted these words broadly, the Commission's mandate was to go
the heart of the Federal Government and review, restructure, and
reduce the scope of governmental activities. 18/

Defenders of the status quo, as it was at that time, considered
that while recommendations could be made in the name of "efficiency,"
the law did not authorize recommending the abolition of substantive
functions. They feared the Commission might venture into the fields
of social security, foreign aid, and veterans' benefits.

For defenders of the Administration, the mandate assigned in the
law was interpreted narrowly. They wanted the Government to continue
what it was doing, but they were willing to concede that it might be
reorganized to perform these functions better. Commissioners critical of the Truman and earlier Roosevelt Administrations, however,
tended to see the "mandate" of the Commission as the "retrenchment"
of the Federal Government.

The terms of this philosophical debate progressively changed
and were ultimately influenced by the results of the 1948 Presidential elections. Hoover's concerns and emphases, however, had
begun to change even prior to the election. As time passed, his
primary goal had shifted from "retrenchment" to the enhancement of
the managerial authority of the President and his departmental
secretaries. This shift in emphasis, begun before the election,
was merely reinforced by the results of the election.

President Truman, although protective of the residuals of the
New Deal, was also sympathetic to the Scientific Management ideals
of traditional public administration. Therefore, he and Herbert
Hoover were not far apart in philosophical terms regarding the
"best" organization of the executive branch. According to
Harold Seidman:

> President Truman had an organizational strategy,
> but it was that supplied to him by the first Hoover
> Commission. The Hoover Commission reports provided
> a conceptual framework for the organizational philoso-
> phy developed by Herbert Hoover during his years as
> President and secretary of commerce, and did not
> stem from Truman's own thinking. There is no evidence,
> however, that the return to orthodoxy symbolized by
> many of the Commission's recommendations was in con-
> flict with Truman's views. 19/

Despite occasional lapses into partisan manuevering, Truman and
Hoover developed a close personal relationship that grew with time
and turned out to be a critical element in whatever success may
be attributed to the Commission. 20/

Commission Staff

A crucial aspect to the success of any study commission is the
quality of the staff. Staffs are rarely neutral, they tend to have
their own political biases and their own professional ambitions.
The report of a commission and its recommendations are likely to be
influenced by the type of persons selected to serve on the staff.
In this respect, the political considerations which entered into
the selection process for key staff positions with the Commission
were not unusual. Peri Arnold recounts how the staff selection
began:

> Upon Hoover's appointment to the new Commission,
> his close political associates began planning for its
> use in a political crusade. Both Hoover and his as-
> sociates realized that the first most pressing job

would be to build a staff. They realized that the
political attitudes of the staff could be the most
important factor in shaping the eventual proposals
of the Commission. Thus staff people were sought who
were free of the 'taint' of the New Deal and the
Roosevelt Democracy. 21/

For the most part, the academic public administrators who had
been involved in staff work for the Brownlow Committee were avoided
although several of them, plus other highly regarded political scientists and public administrators, e.g., Don K. Price, ended up by
making contributions to the Commission effort and in supporting
specific proposals. Generally, the professional staff was a hetero-
geneous group of successful administrators with a predominance
of persons from the private business community.

In the final report to Congress, the Commission listed 74 persons on its own staff. The staff personnel were divided into four
categories: secretarial staff, a group of Commissioners' assistants,
an "administrative staff," and a "central staff." 22/ The secretarial staff of 39 persons provided clerical assistance to the Commission and the task forces. Every member of the Commission was
entitled to one personal assistant, and several members had two assistants. The "administrative staff" consisted of the secretary to
the Commission, a chief of administrative services, and a chief of
personnel, plus one assistant. The "central staff" listed thirteen
names, including the Executive Director, Director of Research,
Director of Public Relations, Editorial Director, and various assistants.

The term "central staff" is a bit misleading in this instance
because the staff did not function as a unit with coordinating responsibilities. Most of the positions were filled late in the Commission's life and were actually aides to the de facto executive
director of the Commission, the Chairman. 23/

There was criticism voiced at the time that Hoover was running
a "one-man show" and that the staff was not being used to best advantage. Commission affairs, it was alleged, suffered from certain
deficiencies of administrative leadership. 24/ The role of the
staff, it appeared to many, was to insure that information was
provided the Chairman, but that the same information was made difficult for individual Commisioners to receive. But even the critics
admitted that the products were produced nearly on schedule and that
the staff contributed to this success.

Task Forces

One of the first decisions made by the Commission was that the
basic work unit would be a "task force." 25/ Twenty-four task forces
were established. 26/ There was no master plan guiding the mandate,
operations, or timing of the reports of the several task forces.
In most instances a task force was headed by a project director, an
individual usually selected by Hoover and accepted by the Commission,
a staff and a task force advisory committee. These advisory committees varied in membership from two to more than thirty, and were
composed of prominent citizens.

> Most committees were advisory, assisting in laying
> out the plan of study and examining the staff finding,
> without giving formal approval of the final task force
> report. Some committees, however, assumed full responsi-
> bility for the assignment, selecting the project director,
> guiding the investigations, and determining the content
> of the report to the Commission. 27/

It is not surprising that the quality of the work performed by
the various task forces differed substantially. In several instances, the individual task force members issued strong dissents
or the report was not published at all. 28/ There were few acade-
micians on the staffs and committees of the task forces. Leaders
prominent in the business community and professional associations
were the primary source for staff and advisory committee personnel.

Five business management firms either made up task forces or
assisted in their work. Two such firms reported directly to the
Commission and did not have to report to supervisory task forces. 29/
In the case of the Personnel Management Task Force, for instance,
they delegated the research function to a management firm and based
their report and recommendations on the data provided by the firm.
The Brookings Institution, without the assistance of a citizens
advisory committee, wrote the task force reports on Transportation
and Welfare.

There was little in the way of coordination among the task
forces. While most of the task forces were structured to study a
function, e.g., Federal Supply, others were structured to study organizations, e.g., Regulatory Agencies. The schedule for receiving
task force reports did not take into account the desirability of
having related reports submitted together. The reports, therefore,
tended to be tentative in nature. Later efforts by the central
staff to systematize and coordinate the efforts of the task forces
were only partially successful. Ferrel Heady concluded:

> Since at no time did the Commission or the
> central staff undertake to provide close and positive
> direction to task force operations, these various

coordinating devices produced slim results. For the
most part, each task force had practically a free
hand in planning its approach, making its investigations,
and formulating its reports; and the unresolved conflicts in substantive recommendations culminating from
this method of operation were thrown directly into the
lap of the Commission when the task force reports were
eventually turned in. 30/

The decision of the Commission to apportion its responsiblity
for studying the various subject fields to task forces was crucial
as it influenced, if not predetermined, the thrust of the analyses
and recommendations the Commission would have before it to consider.
Membership on the task forces tended to be limited to "experts" with
institutional or professional standing in organizations associated
with the business community. Once the membership was chosen, the
recommendations were largely predictable.

Method of Operation

The first meeting of the Commission was held at the White House
on September 29, 1947. Commissioner Brown moved to have Mr. Hoover
elected Chairman, a decision approved unanimously. 31/ Dean Acheson,
a Democrat, was selected as Vice Chairman.

From September 1947 through early June 1948, full Commission
meetings were held once or twice a month. During these early months
much of the time of the Commission was spent in the creation of task
forces, assignment of missions, appointment of staff, and preliminary
investigations. The Commission ceased to meet during the summer of
1948. It was evident that task force assignments were falling behind
schedule so the members requested the Chairman to bring pressure to
bear so that deadlines would be met.

It must be recognized that from the outset Chairman Hoover dominated the Commission and its operations. William Pemberton is typical in his assessment of the contribution of the Chairman to what
soon became known as the Hoover Commission.

Hoover, especially during the first year, dominated
it [the Commission] completely. The sources of his power
were varied. As a former president, he brought with him
prestige that no other commissioner could match. However,
since Hoover had to deal with tough-minded, self-confident
men who would not subordinate themselves even to an ex-
president, other factors also accounted for his control.
Hoover believed that this was his last public service, and
he intended to leave upon it his personal imprint, a resolve
strengthened, no doubt, by his view of the position as an

opportunity to vindicate himself after years of neglect and
scorn. He concentrated all his time and energy on this
task and through sheer hard work he maintained control. 32/

Most of the work of the Commission was done in an office building at 1626 K Street in downtown Washington. Mr. Hoover lived at
the Mayflower Hotel where he would go over the day's program immediately after breakfast and then walk the few blocks to the building, accompanied by his chief aides, Lawrence Richey and Sidney
Mitchell. 33/

In September 1948, the Commission adopted a comprehensive work
schedule. Beginning in October, the Commission met almost weekly,
usually for two or three days at a time. It was during this period
that the Commission began to develop its own collective views,
and its own internal disagreements.

The disagreements among the Commissioners, while genuine, were
not dysfunctional to the group and did not prevent a consensus on
most major issues. The divisions were usually between those attack-
ing the status quo and those defending the Administration, or status
quo. The Administration interests were generally defended by Commissioners Acheson, Rowe, and Pollock, although in no instance was there
a purely partisan split. Every Commissioner wrote at least one dissenting opinion.

In retrospect, a decision made early in the Commission's life
proved crucial to whatever corporate success it enjoyed and to the
direction finally taken in the several reports. Herbert Hoover decided to be his own "task force" for the treatment of the Presidency
in the report on General Management of the Executive Branch. In
discussing this decision with Herbert Emmerich, he stated: "I guess
I'll take that one myself. Who is there who ought to know more
about it?" 34/

Hoover soon realized that he needed assistance in researching
and writing the report. He asked James Webb, then Director of the
Bureau of the Budget, to recommend someone. Webb responded by
suggesting Don K. Price, then with the Public Administration Clearing
House. In addition, Webb provided Hoover with the full support of
the Bureau of the Budget in gaining information and securing the
views of key persons in the White House and Federal bureaucracy.

The decision by Hoover to be responsible for writing the first
task force report was important to the operations of the Commission
because it provided the philosophical basis upon which to evaluate
the other task force reports and recommendations when they were
submitted. It also provided a "model" in terms of content and style.
The ideas may have been as much those of Price and Webb as of Hoover,
but the prose was quintessential Hoover. The sentences were crisp
and to the point although the rules of grammar occasionally suffered
violation. They were written as though for newspaper copy, which
indeed many of them became. 35/

The task forces submitted their reports to the full Commission with recommendations. In most instances, the task force reports were later published separately. The Commission, although it could have written its reports and recommendations without reference to the task force reports, felt constrained to use the task force reports as "working documents" from which deviance tended to require initiative on the part of individual Commissioners. To some degree, therefore, the Commission was constrained in what it could consider or conclude by its own organization and procedure.

The chief advantages of the task force method in conducting research are that it permits a division of labor and the inclusion of more specialists from various fields. These advantages may be dissipated, however, if the supervising element, in this instance the Commission, does not closely oversee the work of its subunits. The task forces occasionally became "limited editions" of the full Commission ready to seek their own will. Charles Aiken commented on this tendency by Commission task forces.

This lack of supervision led some task forces to press for the immediate adoption of their proposals by executive branch agencies instead of devoting their efforts to developing materials solely for the consideration of the Commission. Also some task force leaders, anticipating that their reports to the Commission would be published, regarded their proposals as 'reports to the nation' rather than to the Commission. 36/

For the task force method of operation to work in its best advantage, jurisdictions, assignments, work procedures, and deadlines should be made clear in advance and there should be a systematic review and evaluation of the results. The first Hoover Commission was able to benefit from the task force approach almost in spite of its own laxness in procedures and oversight.

REPORTS

A "single" Commission report was never compiled and forwarded to Congress, rather nineteen separate reports were submitted over three months, the final report being forwarded in May 1949. The reports, relatively brief, were accompanied by appendices based on substantiating materials contained in supporting task force studies. 37/ The decision to submit a series of reports rather than a single comprehensive report was made early in the deliberations. This decision was based partly on the practical problems associated with waiting for all studies to be received and evaluated before beginning a single work, and partly on public relations considerations. Issuing many reports over a period of time afforded more media publicity.

As it happened, the nineteen reports shared a style and brevity that gave the appearance of a single, coordinated report when published together, as they were in 1949 by a private company. 38/

There was no logical pattern by which the reports were grouped or submitted to Congress. Thus, the choice to be made in an attempt to summarize and analyze the report is essentially limited to either discussing them by date of issuance or to develop categories. Ferrel Heady offered a seven-fold classification system which appears useful: management of the executive branch; foreign affairs and defense; natural resources, agriculture, and public works; welfare and labor; Federal business activities; regulatory agencies and commerce; and Federal-State relations. 39/

Management of the Executive Branch

General Management of the Executive Branch

The five reports in this category are generally considered to be the major contribution of the Commission. 40/ The first report, General Management of the Executive Branch, is principally concerned with the Executive Office of the President (EOP) and the problem of departmental management. This initial report was crucial, according to Herbert Emmerich:

> The report on General Management fortunately was
> finished fairly early, and once its main outlines had
> been approved by the commission it provided a general
> point of view which became a connecting thread in
> the subsequent work. The Commission could screen the
> highly diversified, autonomous task force studies in
> the light of a body of doctrine which it had hammered
> out for itself. Thus, it made its job feasible and
> gave greater coherence and unity to the reports that
> followed. 41/

The fundamental organizational assumption underlying the reports of the first Commission was that there was a direct relationship between structure and control. The Commission stated that ". . . we must reorganize the Executive Branch to give it simplicity of structure, the unity of purpose, and the clear line of executive authority that was originally intended." 42/

The Commission, and in this instance the influence of Mr. Hoover is readily apparent, stated its general organizational objectives clearly.

Create a more orderly grouping of the functions
of Government into major departments and agencies
under the President.

Establish a clear line of control from the
President to those department and agency heads and
from them to their subordinates with correlative
responsibility from these officials to the president,
cutting through the barriers which have in many
cases made bureaus and agencies partially independent
of the Chief Executive.

Permit the operating departments and agencies
to administer for themselves a larger share of the
routine administrative services, under strict supervision and in conformity with high standards. 43/

This set of objectives constituted both a set of doctrines to
guide the entire Commission effort and a clarion call for an administrative system under the managerial control of the President. Although never mentioned by name, the influence of the 1937 Brownlow
Committee report is unmistakable. 44/ For various reasons, however,
the Commission decided to rely for historical precedence and legiti-
macy upon the Founding Fathers and their intention to promote a
"vigorous executive."

As a statement of administrative philosophy, the goals of the
first Hoover Commission were definitely in the tradition of the
Scientific Management movement and of earlier reform efforts. 45/
Hoover wanted to achieve "economy and efficiency" in the Federal
Government and he believed that this was possible only if the
executive branch was organized hierarchically with a strong President as administrative manager. While both these concepts had
long had their adherents, there were few in the body politic who
held both views passionately at the same time.

The doctrine underlying most of the recommendations was that
responsibility for making policy and setting standards ought to be
centralized in the President and department secretaries, rather than
being devolved to the agency level. The Commission criticized the
tendency towards dispersing functions to independent agencies and
called for a renewed, hierarchical administrative structure.

The section titled Departmental Management was short. The
Commission believed that the departmental system had deteriorated
because Congress, and sometimes the President, had departed from the
norm of the integrated administrative system envisioned by the
Constitution.

The Congress, and sometimes the President, have
set up a maze of independent agencies reporting directly
to the President; and the Congress frequently has fixed

by statute the internal organization of departments and
agencies and has given authority directly to subordinate
officers. As a result, instead of being a unified
organization, responsible to the executive direction of
the President and accountable to the Congress for use of
the power and funds granted by law, the executive branch
is a chaos of bureaus and subdivisions.

The responsibility, the vigor of executive leadership,
and the unity of administration of the executive branch
as planned by the Constitution must be restored. 46/

The recommendations were for grouping agencies into departments
"as nearly as possible by major purposes." Department secretaries
should be given full responsibility and authority for the conduct
of their department. There should be decentralization into the
operating agencies of such services as accounting, budgeting, re-
cruiting and managing of personnel. And finally, department heads
should be given increased staff support. The Commission concluded,
in a rather off-handed fashion: "We recommend that these various
agencies be consolidated into about one-third of the present
number." 47/

The Commission was generally pleased with the development of the
Executive Office of the President (EOP) although they called for a
new Office of Personnel to be headed by a director who would also
serve as chairman of the Civil Service Commission. They also recommended that heads of EOP staff offices be exempt from Senate confirmation. The Council of Economic Advisers (CEA) should be replaced
by an Office of Economic Adviser headed by a single administrator.
The National Security Council staff should become formally, as well
as in practice, part of the White House Office. There were proposals to strengthen the Bureau of the Budget as the "managerial arm
of the President."

It is interesting to note that the Commission did not make any
recommendations designed to convert the Cabinet into a more cohe-
sive policy developing unit with a degree of collective responsibility. 48/ "The Cabinet as a body," the Commission concluded, "is
not an effective council of advisers to the President and it does not
have a collective responsibility for Administration policies. The
Cabinet members, chosen to direct specialized operating departments,
are not all fitted to advise him on every subject." 49/

The Commission recommended that the President be given permanent
authority to submit reorganization plans to effectuate changes in
structure and that such plans should not be restricted by limitations
or exemptions. "Once the limiting and exempting process is begun,"
the Commission asserted, "it will end the possibility of achieving
really substantial results."

But, in saying this, the Commission should not be
understood as giving sweeping endorsement to any and all
reorganization plans. It does believe that the safe-
guard against unwise reorganization plans lies both in
the sound exercise of the President's discretion and
in the reserved power in the Congress by concurrent
resolution to disapprove any proposed plan. 50/

The report on General Management of the Executive Branch constituted a clear, concise statement of many of the orthodox principles
of public administration as applied in a practical sense to the executive branch. As a reading of subsequent reports indicates, however, the Commission encountered difficulty in applying these principles to all the fields under study.

Budget and Accounting

The Commission concluded in its report on Budget and Accounting
that the budget of the executive branch was an inadequate document.
They rejected the line item approach to budgeting. "We recommend
that the whole budgetary concept of the Federal Government should
be refashioned by the adoption of a budget based upon functions,
activities and projects: this we designate as a 'performance budget.'" 51/ The objective was to center both congressional and executive attention on the function or activity being performed, not on
the purchase of things or salaries of employees. In addition, the
Commission proposed the segregation of capital from current outlays.

The Commission believed that the Bureau of the Budget 52/ ought
to be much closer to the White House Office and that there be "closer
relations" between constituent units of the Bureau and the White
House staff. The Bureau would remain, however, the "permanent government" to assist the political executives. The Commission further
appeared to favor an "item veto" for the President who "should have
authority to reduce expenditures under appropriations, if the purposes intended by the Congress are still carried out." 53/

The Commission recommended that an Accountant General be established in the Treasury with responsibility for accounting and reporting throughout the executive branch. The accounting methods and procedures to be applied, however, would be subject to the approval of
the Comptroller General. 54/ This recommendation inspired strong
reservations and was never implemented. 55/

Office of General Services

"Three major internal activities of the Federal Government now suffer from a lack of central direction," according to the Commission. These activities were supply, records management, and the operation and maintenance of public buildings. The need for central authority in these areas was documented by the Commission. The answer to this problem, in the opinion of the Commission, was to establish an Office of General Services under an Administrator, a recommendation that later came to fruition in form of the General Services Administration. 56/

The proposed Office of General Services would have a Bureau of Federal Supply, a Records Management Bureau, to include the National Archives, and a Public Buildings Administration.

Personnel Management

The Commission wanted to strengthen the personnel policies and management of the Federal Government. It believed that the weaknesses of the civil service system were largely attributable to excessive centralization of personnel transactions in the Civil Service Commission, unsophisticated recruitment processes, and inadequate compensation. 57/

In its report on Personnel Management, the Commission offered a large number of recommendations, many of which constituted a latter-day menu of civil service "reformers." The Brownlow Committee had recommended the abolition of the three-member Civil Service Commission in favor of a single personnel administrator. The Hoover Commission retreated somewhat from this recommendation and indicated its approval of continuing the Commission in its present form although the Chairman would be assigned responsibility for the administrative work of the Commission. 58/

With respect to compensation, the rates for blue collar, sub-professional, and clerical jobs should be adjusted to "prevailing locality, area, or industry pay differentials." Later, " . . . immediate consideration should be given to providing adequate salaries for top civil service employees with exceptional professional, scientific, technical, and administrative qualifications." 59/ Further, in more specific terms, the Commission endorsed the veterans' preference program, recommended the loosening of the "rule of three" requirement for appointing officers, and advocated changes in the regulations governing reductions in force.

Although the Commission did not recommend the creation of a senior executive service as a means to encourage more mobility among

top civil servants, it did recommend that departments pay more attention to encouraging executive mobility.

Treasury Department

The Commission sought to make the Department of the Treasury the
"real fiscal center of the Government." 60/ Ten recommendations to
implement this goal were submitted, including several recommendations
to transfer agencies and functions both to and from the Department.
For instance, it was recommended that the United States Coast Guard
be transferred from the Treasury to the Department of Commerce while
supervision of operations of the Reconstruction Finance Corporation,
Federal Deposit Insurance Corporation, and the Export-Import Bank
be vested in the Treasury Secretary. By and large, the recommendations proved controversial and unacceptable to many of the leaders
in the executive branch and Congress. 61/

Foreign Affairs and Defense

National Security Organization

In 1947, after more than a year of debate within the Administration, the President submitted legislation to Congress to create a
National Military Establishment. The bill called for, among other
things, the continuation of the individual branches of the armed services, their subordination to a single, civilian Secretary and the
creation of a National Security Council chaired by the President. 62/

The concept of a National Security Council (NSC) derived from
the Eberstadt Report, a series of studies with recommendations com-
missioned in the summer of 1945 by the Secretary of the Navy, James
Forrestal, and prepared under the direction of Ferdinand Eberstadt. 63/ Initially, the Navy saw the Council as a kind of "war
cabinet" which would obviate the need to fully integrate the services
into a single Department. In a sense, the Navy's concept of the
National Security Council was that a "kind of substitute Secretary
of Defense." The underlying assumption was that persons responsible
for a segment of defense could meet together and produce a whole,
coordinated defense policy. Certain political realities, Paul
Hammond asserted, imposed themselves upon the new Council. "Once the
NSC was established, the divergent purposes which had brought it into
being all yielded, of necessity, to one: the Presidential purpose.
For while the NSC could be less, it could be no more than what the
President wanted it to be, if he knew his own mind." 64/

The first appraisal of the newly created NSC was conducted less than a year after its creation by the Hoover Commission's Task Force on National Security Organization. Initially, Secretary Forrestal, a member of the Commission, had been opposed to a Commission review as "premature." His opposition faded, however, when Ferdinand Eberstadt was appointed as head of the Task Force. 65/

It had been originally assumed in 1947 that the NSC would be the source of most policy initiatives in the military establishment. By November 1948, however, it was evident that the NSC would not be able to serve in this role. Part of the problem, according to Hammond, was that if the Council became the source of policy initiatives in its own right, then to that degree the Presidential Office would be diminished.

President Truman answered a fundamental question of defense policy-making concerning the NSC by making it a practice not to sit with the NSC during its first three years, until the Korean War began. Forrestal had anticipated that he would not attend simply because the burdens of the Presidency made the delegation of his responsibilities necessary. Yet, that was not the reason. Rather, it was because Truman felt his presence on the NSC might imply a delegation of authority which he did not intend. 66/

In part because the NSC had not lived up to the expectations of its promoters, the Commission turned to other options. They sought unification rather than federation, and to strengthen the Department and the Secretary. It was recommended that the Secretary be given by Congress authority to reorganize and control his organization, and "that separate authorities to component subordinates be eliminated." 67/ A "performance budget" should be required of all units.

The Commission recommended that the Secretary of Defense have full authority, subject only to the President and the Congress, to establish internal policies and programs. It further recommended that service secretaries be deprived of their privilege of appealing over the head of the Defense Secretary to the President and that the Secretary be the sole person reporting to the President. 68/

The Commission wanted "vigorous steps" to be taken to improve the Central Intelligence Agency. They also recommended that "emergency plans for civilian and industrial mobilization be completed promptly." The conclusion of the Commission report read: "These provisions should insure the full control and accountability of the military to civilian control by establishing the Secretary of Defense as the principal assistant to the President in military matters, responsible to him and to the Congress for the conduct, efficiency, and economy of the National Military Establishment." 69/ The Commission's recommendations were in large part incorporated into the National Security Act Amendments of 1949 (63 Stat. 203). 70/

Foreign Affairs

In its report to Congress on Foreign Affairs management, the Commission described the complexity of conducting foreign affairs in the post World War II era with emphasis on what it considered excessive dispersion of responsibilities among departments and agencies. Given this dispersion of foreign affairs responsibilities, what role should be played by the President, Department of State, and the Congress in coordinating these varied activities?

The recommendations of the Commission took the form of "principles." "Neither this report, nor that of the supporting task force, purports to be a complete 'blueprint' covering the major possible applications of these principles." 71/

Legislation which grants new foreign affairs powers of an executive nature otherwise than to the President or to an established executive department or agency, the Commission asserted, will normally cause serious difficulty for efficient administration. 72/ In this plea for integration of foreign policy structure and administration, the Commission recommended to Congress that it forego the temptation to assign in legislation the administration of programs and policies to subordinate units. Hierarchical lines of authority and responsibility should be reinforced.

Cabinet level committees, with their memberships and assignments fixed by the President, should be encouraged in foreign policy areas where several departments and agencies are jointly involved. These committees, however, should not "supplant the State Department as a staff arm of the President, and the State Department in this role should be the major coordinating force within the executive branch on foreign affairs matters." 73/

With respect to the State Department, the Commission concluded:

The State Department should concentrate on obtaining definition of proposed objectives for the United States in foreign affairs, on formulating proposed policies in conjunction with other departments and agencies to achieve those objectives, and on recommending the choice and timing of the use of various instruments to carry out foreign policies so formulated. 74/

The State Department, as a rule, should not be given responsibility for the operation of specific programs, whether overseas or domestic. The traditional functions of the State Department; representation, reporting, and negotiation, should be continued and improved. Reorganization of the State Department to enhance the command role of the Secretary should be assisted by a revised organization of under and assistant secretaries.

With respect to the Foreign Service Officer Corps, the Commission recommended that it be amalgamated with the regular career service personnel into a Foreign Affairs Service administered separately from the general Civil Service system. 75/ As it happened, this was the only recommendation in the Commission report on Foreign Affairs, a report generally praised, 76/ not to be implemented.

Natural Resources, Agriculture, and Public Works

Department of the Interior

Three task forces on natural resources were created by the Commission: Natural Resources; Agriculture; and Public Works. When the Commission received the reports of these task forces, it attempted to evaluate them collectively so that the full Commission's recommendations would be internally consistent. The Commission was only moderately successful in this endeavor as the task forces had carried on their deliberations based on very different and contradictory premises. Conflicts of long-standing erupted once again and the sides found compromise nearly impossible.

The Commission recommended that the Department of the Interior be reorganized 77/ and that the Army Corps of Engineers and the Bureau of Reclamation be consolidated into a Water Development and Use Service. 78/ "One of the major reasons," the Commission argued, "for grouping these agencies into the Department of the Interior is the elimination of disastrously wasteful conflict." 79/ The existing organizational arrangement for Federal water resource programs violated virtually every element of orthodox administrative theory. As President, Herbert Hoover in 1932 had proposed that the civil functions of the Corps of Engineers be transferred to the Department of the Interior, but his proposal was rejected by the House.

Various scholars over the years have been critical of the Army Corps of Engineers and its alleged ability to impose its own definition of proper water resources utilization upon other political actors. 80/ This criticism had reached something of a peak during the period when the first Hoover Commission was meeting. The reason that no major reorganization of the Corps of Engineers had taken place, and has not to this day, is answerable in one word; Congress. A substantial number, possibly a majority, of Members of Congress have never been persuaded that they ought to relinquish the special relationship they have with the Corps. Writing in 1980, Harold Seidman observed:

> Almost every objective observer has confirmed the
> Hoover Commission's findings that the existing sharing
> of water resource responsibilities among Interior,

Agriculture, and the U.S. Army Corps of Engineers has
resulted in poor planning, overlapping and duplication,
working at cross purposes, and wasteful competition.
Entrenched interests within the bureaucracy and outside
community constitute major obstacles to needed reorganization. But these obstacles would not be insuperable,
if the schism in the executive branch did not have its
counterpart in the Congress.

Congressional organization and executive branch
organization with respect to water resources are so
closely interlinked that they cannot be considered
separately. Control over project authorization and
funding are the essence of congressional power. 81/

The report on the Interior Department acknowledged, but took
little counsel from, the report of the Public Works task force headed
by the irrepressible Robert Moses of New York. This task force had
recommended that a comprehensive Federal Works Department be created
consisting of an extraordinary array of agencies, tied together because of their involvement with engineering. In this instance, the
task force was recommending that the organizing principle should be
work process rather than function performed or clientele ser-
viced. 82/

In what appeared to be a belated "bone" to the Public Works task
force, the Commission agreed to recommend the establishment of a
Board of Impartial Analysis for Engineering and Architectural Projects 83/ to advise and report to the President and the Congress on
the public and economic value of project proposals by agencies. The
Board would consist of five presidentially appointed members with
recognized engineering abilities, or to use the task force's more
colorful language, "the seagreen incorruptibles of the engineering
profession." The Board would be located in the Executive Office of
the President. 84/

The Commission recommended that the Department be reorganized
into four Services: Water Development and Use; Building Construction; Mineral Resources; and Recreation. 85/ While the Commission
was critical of the current administration of mineral resources, it
is interesting to note, in light of later events, that there was no
discussion of petroleum as a natural resource. 86/

Congress approved recommendations designed to improve the internal administration of the Department, as stated originally in the
report on general management, and two minor functional transfers to
the Department were accomplished by reorganization plan. Otherwise,
the major recommendations of the Commission were found by Congress to
be unacceptable.

Department of Agriculture

In the Commission's opinion, the Department of Agriculture had become too decentralized, "causing an unnecessary diffusion of authority. The Department has grown to its present size without sufficient integration of its parts and with considerable overlap and duplication. It is a loose confederation of independent bureaus and agencies." 87/ To overcome this deficiency, the Commission recommended various measures to strengthen the Secretary and integrate the functions of the Department. While the recommendations were couched in neutral, managerial terminology, the political significance of these recommendations in terms of altering political relationships was not lost on many in Congress and they balked, thereby jeopardizing many of the recommendations. 88/

The Commission was dissatisfied with the field services of the Department and recommended that "except in the most unusual circumstances, activities that are services to individual farmers should be administered in the field by departmental employees through offices based on States as units." 89/

Regulatory functions relating to food products should be "transferred to the Department of Agriculture and that those relating to other products be placed under a reorganized Drug Bureau administered by the public health agency." 90/

After a recitation of costs involved in the "long and wasteful conflict and overlap between certain soil conservation, range, forest, and allied services due to the division of their functions between the Department of Agriculture and the Department of the Interior," the Commission recommended that these functions be consolidated in one department. The issue, however, remained; to which department should they be assigned? "The task force on agricultural activities urgently recommends that these consolidated activities be placed in the Department of Agriculture. Our task force on natural resources urgently recommends that they be transferred to the Department of the Interior or its successor." 91/

> This Commission believes that logic and public policy require that major land agencies be grouped in the Department of Agriculture. It recommends that the land activities of the Department of the Interior, chiefly the public domain (except mineral questions) and the Oregon and California revested lands be transferred to the Department or Agriculture and that the water development activities (except the local farm supply of water) be transferred to the Department of the Interior. 92/

The results of the Commission's efforts at compromise were that water resources management would be assigned to Interior while land use management would be assigned to Agriculture. In specific terms, the Forest Service would remain in Agriculture

while the Bureau of Land Management would be transferred out of
Interior and into the Department of Agriculture.

Efforts to reframe many of the recommendations in acceptable
legislative language came to naught. In sum, therefore, few of
the recommendations of the Commission respecting the Department
of Agriculture were adopted.

Welfare and Labor

Under the general heading of welfare and labor are to be found
four Commission reports: Veterans' Affairs; Department of Labor;
Social Security, Education and Indian Affairs; and Medical Activities.

Veterans' Affairs

The recommendations of the Commission's report on Veterans' Affairs were fairly lean. The Commission first noted the size of the
Veterans' Administration (VA); the agency would spend more in 1950
than any other Federal agency save the National Military Establishment and the Treasury Department. "While the Administrator of the
Veterans' Affairs," the Commission observed, "enjoys broader administrative discretion in organizing his agency than most important
governmental officials, serious internal organizational defects still
exist." 93/ The defects included "conflicting lines of authority"
between Washington and the field units, too many headquarters units
based on process rather than program, and too many regulations.

The Commission recommended that "the Administrator of Veterans'
Affairs reorganize his office in Washington in accordance with the
general principles suggested in our first report." 94/ The VA should
be "given authority to establish a system of certification for all
educational institutions which are not 'accredited institutions' in
that they have not been approved by recognized accrediting organizations . . . ." 95/

On the program level, the Commission recommended that all functions relating to veterans' insurance be consolidated and incorporated into a Veterans' Life Insurance Corporation. 96/ And second,
that the veterans' housing loan guaranty program be transferred to
the Housing and Home Finance Agency, with the Veterans' Administration retaining the certification of eligibility function. 97/

Department of Labor

In its brief report on the Department of Labor, the Commission concluded: "In general, it can be said that the Department of Labor has lost much of its significance and should have restored to it the many agencies we have here recommended. This would make for greater efficiency in the Government." 98/

The Commission began its report by noting that the Department had "been steadily denuded of functions at one time established within it." As with reports on other departments, the Commission recommended that the Department of Labor be reorganized to increase Secretarial authority and that various procedures be introduced, e.g., decentralized personnel recruitment.

Several agencies were recommended for transfer to the Department. From the Federal Security Agency would come the Bureau of Employees' Compensation, Employee's Compensation Appeals Board, and the Bureau of Employment Security. It was recommended that the Selective Service System, an independent agency, be transferred to the Department. 99/ A number of other minor functions, e.g., determination of minimum wages for seamen (from U.S. Maritime Commission), were also recommended for transfer.

In the Department of Labor report there were eight recommendations. They were implemented for the most part with two notable exceptions, both of which were considered and rejected. Congress decided to keep the Selective Service System independent and to reject the proposed transfer from the Maritime Administration of the Department of Commerce to the Department of Labor the functions relative to the determination of minimum wages for merchant seaman on privately owned, subsidized vessels.

Social Security, Education, and Indian Affairs

The Commission began its report with the recommendation that a "new Department to administer the functions set forth in this report be created and headed by a Cabinet Officer." 100/ The name of this new Department, however, was not provided. It was to be built upon the base of the existing Federal Security Agency although a number of agencies and functions would be transferred from the FSA prior to its elevation to departmental status.

There was no task force, per se, appointed to study the general welfare area. Rather, the Brookings Institution was contracted and wrote a comprehensive report for the Commission consisting of six parts: General Question of Departmentalism; Health; Education; Employment; Relief and Social Security; and Recreation. Brookings

took no formal position on whether there ought to be several small
unifunctional departments or a single, large multifunctional department. The thrust of their analysis, however, seemed to favor
the several department option.

The Department proposed by the Commission would have three
principal responsibilities: social security and related programs;
education; and Indian affairs. Health functions in the FSA would
be transferred out. 101/ The Commission specifically rejected
the idea of creating a separate new department for education. 102/

Among the other recommendations of the Commission with respect
to welfare were one to divest the Children's Bureau of grant
functions and shift the Bureau to a general staff capacity to the
Secretary, 103/ and another to continue the educational programs
pretty much as they were then being performed.

With respect to Indians, the Commission accepted the dominant
philosophy of the time that Federal policy should encourage the
integration of Indians and part-Indians into the larger society.

> Our Task Force on Indian Affairs, supported by
> a considerable body of thought both inside and outside
> the Government, advocates progressive measures to
> integrate the Indians into the rest of the population
> as the best solution to 'the Indian Problem.' In the
> opinion of the Commission this policy should be the
> keystone of the organization and the activities of
> the Federal Government in the field of Indian Affairs. 104/

The Commission went further to recommend that "pending achievement of the goal of complete integration," the administration of
social programs for Indians be progressively transferred to State
governments. And finally, the Commission recommended that the
Bureau of Indian Affairs be transferred from the Department of the
Interior to the new Department. 105/

The Commission provided 17 specific recommendations, the most
important one being that to create a new Department to administer
the major functions of Federal social security and educational
services. The question of whether or not a Department ought to be
created out of the Federal Security Agency and what agencies and
functions ought to be assigned had been discussed in Congress for
a number of years. Following the submission of the Citizens
Committee bill to implement the full recommendation of the Commission, the President submitted Reorganization Plan No. 1 of
1949, to create a Department of Welfare. Its provisions were
practically identical to the Citizens Committee bill, but it did
not include the transfer of Indian affairs. This Plan was rejected as was a similar proposal (Reorganization Plan No. 27 of
1950) a year later. Many of the Commission's other specific recommendations were enacted by statute or implemented by Executive action.

Medical Activities

Initially, the Commission instructed the Task Force on Medical Activities to assume that medical activities then residing in the Federal Security Agency would be continued under the leadership of a new department. 106/ Later, the task force was requested to consider the advisibility of placing medical service functions in a single, independent agency. The task force subsequently strongly recommended a separate United Medical Administration. 107/

A divided Commission recommended the establishment of a United Medical Administration (UMA) into which would be consolidated most of the large-scale activities of the Federal Government in the fields of medical care, medical research, and public health. 108/ The UMA would provide the major part of military medical services domestically. "The Veterans' Administration would continue to certify patients for treatment and would determine disability, ratings, etc., but the UMA would look after veterans' medical care." 109/

"This unification," according to the Commission, "does not contemplate the creation of an additional Government agency, in the usual sense. It proposes uniting the facilities and resources of existing agencies." 110/

The proposed UMA would be headed by a presidentially appointed administrator, to be "assisted by an advisory board, consisting of the Surgeons General of the Army and Navy, the Air Surgeon, and the Administrator of Veterans' Affairs, or his representatives. This board shall advise the Administrator on policies. Thus, we propose a unity of services in the national interest, rather than separate services to special groups." 111/

At the request of the chairman of the Senate Committee on Government Operations, attorneys for the Hoover Commission prepared a bill for implementing the Commission's recommendations. In hearings before the Senate Committee on Labor and Public Works, the Federal Security Administrator and the Administrator of Veterans' Affairs voiced strong opposition to the bill. In view of the concerted opposition, no action was taken. A subsequent bill with a similar, although more modest, objective also failed to gather the necessary support, even among the medical associations.

Federal Business Activities

Federal Business Enterprises

Federal business activities are discussed in two reports; Federal Business Enterprises and the Post Office. The former report

turned out to be one of the most controversial. Controversy was to
be expected if for no other reason than the fact that so many topics
were included under the rubric of Federal business enterprises. A-
gencies engaged in lending, guaranteeing, and insurance activities,
electric power and irrigation and miscellaneous business enterprises
were included. 112/

In 1949, there were about 100 business-type enterprises the Federal Government owned or in which it was financially involved. These
enterprises were either specially chartered by Congress in accordance
with the Government Corporation Control Act of 1945, or were unincorporated enterprises administered under older departmental forms.
After a recitation of the variations then present in corporate char-
ters and financial systems, and some of the unpleasant consequences
resulting therefrom, the Commission made several recommendations.

The Commission, for example, recommended amending the Government
Corporation Control Act so "that borrowing powers, Government liability for their obligations, and budgetary presentation be made uni-
form for like classes of loans and securities." Further, that Congress adopt a policy to regulate the disposition of surpluses from
these corporations. And finally, "in order to establish a consistent practice among corporations, that all corporations, in determining the cost of construction undertaken by them, include a charge
for interest on capital expended during the period of construction." 113/

Certain unincorporated business enterprises were singled out
(Washington National Airport and Alaska Railroad) as examples of
straightline business activities that ought to be incorporated "so
as to secure greater flexibility in management and simpler accounting, budgeting, and auditing methods." 114/

The Commission came out strongly against direct lending to individuals and enterprises because of the possibilities of favoritism.
"It invites political and private pressures, or even corruption."
There was a recommendation that "all housing activities be placed in
one agency under a single administrator . . . ." 115/ Farm credit
enterprises were reviewed and it was recommended that some should be
consolidated into single system with the gradual privitization of the
enterprise.

The future of the Farmers Home Administration (FmHA) generated
considerable controversy among Commission members. It was an undeni-
able fact that the FmHA's functions overlapped, but not necessarily
duplicated, the functions of two other competing agencies, the Farm
Credit Administration and the Agricultural Extension Service. "Our
task force on Agriculture," the Commission noted, "has strongly urged
that the activity of the Farmers Home Administration be reduced. Our
task force on Government lending strongly recommends that this agency
be liquidated at once." Notwithstanding its agreement with the
criticisms leveled at the FmHA as an agency, the Commission stated

that "it appears . . . that there is a valid service to be performed in this field for good tenant and other farmers. It should be
put on a sounder basis." 116/

The Commission recommended that the FmHA be liquidated and that
its functions be transferred. Continuing, the Commission recommended
that a "modest Government corporation be set up under the Agricultural Credit Administration" (Farm Credit Administration). Tenant farmers would then make their loan applications to the Land Bank following, for the most part, criteria established by the Land Bank. The
new "modest corporation" would guarantee a second mortgage loan to be
made by the Land Bank, making total loans up to 90 percent of the appraised value. Guidance and advice to the potential borrower would
be provided by the Department of Agriculture through the Extension
Service. In the opinion of the majority of the Commissioners, such
a reorganization would eliminate a case of overlapping in programs
and result in savings for the taxpayers.

Vigorous dissents were filed by Commissioners Acheson, Pollock,
Rowe, Manasco, and Forrestal on the question of the fate of the
FmHA. The thrust of the dissents was that it was incorrect to judge
the FmHA and its programs as a "business activity." "It was the intent of Congress that the Farmers Home Administration should furnish
a special kind of credit assistance to farmers who constitute margi-
nal risks. The purpose of the Farmers Home Administration is to make
'good' tenant farmers out of 'poor' tenant farmers, and not to re-
strict credit to 'good' tenant farmers who can probably obtain credit
from other sources." 117/

Although the Commission discussed this particular reorganization
in rather dry language, clearly stressing the values of "economy and
efficiency" as justification for abolishing the FmHA and transferring
its functions to two other competing agencies, it was generally understood at the time that this recommendation was highly charged in
political terms. 118/ Congress never implemented the Commission's
recommendations regarding the Farmers Home Administration.

There was more controversy over the Reconstruction Finance Corporation (RFC). The task force on Lending Agencies recommended the
liquidation of the Corporation and the substitution of guarantees by
the Government, operating through the Federal Reserve Banks, of loans
by commercial banks. The Commission, however, demurred from this
recommendation believing it "preferable that the Corporation be
reorganized to guarantee loans by commercial banks." 119/ In the
report on the Treasury Department, the Commission had recommended
that the RFC be placed under the supervision of the Secretary of the
Treasury. 120/

"We suggest," the Commission continued, "that the Congress consider the creation of a system of National Mortgage Discount Banks to

provide real estate mortgage discount facilities for all private
lending agencies over the entire real property field. This might
include the present Federal Home Loan Banks." 121/ The defense of
this proposal rested on the belief that if such a bank was created,
the need for Government agencies would be gradually reduced. "Private lending institutions would be more active if they felt that,
when under pressure, they could render their assets liquid."

The Commission once again entered the quagmire of water resources use and the conflict between flood control and navigation
versus irrigation and power. After describing the numerous multiple
use water projects then completed or under development, the Commission simply stated:

> Individual members of this Commission have different
> points of view as to the organizational and administrative
> recommendations of the Government's electric power and ir-
> rigation enterprises. Individual suggestions are given
> at the end of the report. 122/

Ferrel Heady, in evaluating the work of the first Hoover Commission, concluded that in this one field, the Commission "fell apart at
the seams." 123/

There were 23 recommendations in this report, 15 of them dealing
with general operations of Government corporations and with housing
enterprises, four with farm-credit enterprises, with the remaining
four proposing specific legislative actions. All the recommendations
dealt with legislative policy. They were "so broad and involved that
the attorneys for the Hoover Commission did not submit a draft bill
to put the recommendations into specific legislative proposals, as
requested by the chairman (Senator McClellan) of this committee
(Senate Government Operations Committee) and no specific drafts were
compiled by the Citizens Committee for the Hoover Report for implementation of the report." 124/

Notwithstanding a number of rejections of proposals to alter
Federal banking and loan institutions, legislative actions in 1950
and 1951 resulted in implementing many of the concepts embodied in
the Commission report, if not their exact provisions. Attributing
credit for concepts is difficult at best. In many instances, ideas
that found fruition in laws or administrative action at this time
had been advocated for many years with the Hoover Commission merely
being one of the sources offering its imprimatur. Also, many of
the recommendations in this report were duplicated, in part, by
recommendations to be found in other reports, thereby further compli-
cating the attribution and approval measurements.

Post Office

The Commission's report on the Post Office was short and noncontroversial. 125/ In its usual pithy style, the Commission described what was "wrong" with the Post Office Department. "The administrative structure is obsolete and overcentralized. A maze of out-moded laws, regulations, and traditions freezes progress and stifles proper administration. Although the Post Office is a business-type establishment, it lacks the freedom and flexibility essential to good business operation." 126/

A reorganized Post Office might be able to eliminate the chronic deficits. The Commission recommended that while the Post Office remain an executive department, the Postmaster General not be an official of a political party nor should the Post Office be used as a patronage haven. "We recommend that the confirmation of Postmasters by the Senate should be abolished." 127/

Although the Commission did not advocate a corporate status for the Post Office, it did recommend that it be viewed more like a business and that its budgetary, accounting, and auditing processes should reflect this business orientation. Further, the Commission believed that the Post Office should charge rates that would make it self-sufficient. 128/ Of the nine recommendations submitted by the Commission, six were implemented. The remaining three were considered by Congress, but were not approved.

Regulatory Commissions and Commerce

Regulatory Commissions

With respect to the independent regulatory commissions, the Commission's approach differed from that of the earlier President's Committee on Administrative Management (Brownlow Committee). The Brownlow Committee had been harsh in its judgment of the regulatory commissions referring to them as the "headless fourth branch of Government" and recommended that they be abolished and their functions transferred to executive departments. 129/ In the departments, these functions would be divided between an administrative section, under the direction of a single administrator who would be a career civil servant, and a judicial section which would function independently in making regulatory determinations.

The Hoover Commission began with the assumption that the independent regulatory commissions were likely to remain independent of the executive branch and therefore concentrated on administrative

issues. 130/ The task force concluded that there were adequate opportunities for the President to exert influence on the commissions
without eliminating their independent status. The task force did
take issue, however, with the Brookings Institution study for the
Hoover Commission on transportation which had recommended that a
single transportation regulatory agency be set up into which the
Interstate Commerce Commission, the Civil Aeronautics Board, and
the Maritime Commission would be merged. The task force contended
that the fields were sufficiently distinctive to warrant separate
agencies. 131/

Deviating little from the task force report, the full Commission
limited its recommendations principally to administrative matters.
The full Commission recommended "that all administrative responsibility be vested in the chairman of the commission." 132/ There was
concern to upgrade salaries and status of the regulatory commission
members and their staffs on the assumption that competent personnel
can often overcome institutional weaknesses. The Commission did accept the view that the regulatory commissions were under the Bureau
of the Budget for administrative purposes, to include budgetary and
legislative clearance. 133/ There were several recommendations reflecting the view of the Commission that functions of a "purely executive" character ought to be removed from the commissions and assigned to regular agencies, mostly in the Department of Commerce.
Ten of the Commissioners upheld the task force conclusion that a
single transportation regulatory commission was not desirable. 134/

The full Commission did not adopt the task force recommendation
that the President ought to designate commission chairman and that
they serve at his pleasure. This authority had been considered
critical to the task force's effort to increase the degree of general
executive responsibility for regulatory administration. 135/ Its
omission, therefore, was read as a sign that the Commission was
satisfied with the status quo in regulatory commission independence. 136/

The broad objective of the 12 recommendations in the report on
regulatory commissions was to support the independent status of the
commissions while improving their internal administrative structure.
These recommendations reflected the Commission's acceptance of the
then dominant philosophy that the public interest was best served by
regulating prices and entry into the market rather than encouraging
competition.

The President submitted eight reorganization plans in 1950 to
vest administrative responsibility for day-to-day operations in each
of the respective commission chairmen. Congress rejected three
of the plans (No. 7, Interstate Commerce; No. 11, Federal Communi-
cations Commission; and No. 12, National Labor Relations Board).

Department of Commerce

    With respect to the Department of Commerce, there was no task
force appointed. 137/ The Commission itself wrote the report and
emphasized that "the major purpose of the Department, as originally
established by the Congress, was to embrace the activities of the
Government in the development of industry, transportation, and commerce. However, a number of these functions have been placed else-
where in the Government structure and the transportation activities
have been scattered over many parts of the executive branch." 138/

    The Commission sought to restore to the Department some of its
original mission and status by recommending the transfer to it of
various agencies and functions. The administrative and promotional
activities of the Maritime Commission, the Civil Aeronautics Board,
and the Interstate Commerce Commission would be transferred. The
National Advisory Committee for Aeronautics, presently independent,
would be transferred. Also to be transferred to the Department
would be the Public Roads Administration, Office of Defense
Transportation, Coast Guard and certain functions of the Bureau of
Customs. Finally, the Division of Commercial Fisheries was tar-
geted for transfer from the Department of the Interior. 139/

    There followed the now usual recommendations regarding the
internal reorganization of the Department to enhance the authority
of the Secretary, the institution of a "performance budget," and
the decentralization of the personnel recruitment and procurement.
A "model" department was described and diagrammed.

    The Commission disagreed with its task force on transportation
which had recommended the creation of a separate Department of Transportation. 140/ "It would be quite inadvisable for the Federal
Government to set up a department which would be devoted entirely to
the problems of one industry." 141/ Instead, the Commission recommended that there be established in the Department of Commerce a
grouping of all major nonregulatory transportation activities.

    Congress found most of the recommendations respecting the De-
partment of Commerce to be unacceptable on the grounds that they
required major shifts in legislative policy. The departmental
management recommendations were accepted as were the transfer of
the Public Roads Administration from the General Services Administration and the incorporation of the independent U.S. Maritime
Commission into the Department as the Maritime Administration. 142/
Otherwise, there was widespread opposition to the proposal to
transfer to Commerce all the "nonregulatory transport activities"
from various agencies. The general view appeared to be that the
promotional and administrative activities in the field of transportation were integral and supportive to the regulatory functions
of existing agencies and ought not be separated. And finally,
the proposal to transfer the National Advisory Committee for

Aeronautics (NACA) and its research facilities was vigorously opposed by the NACA leadership and the scientific community, so
Congress left it independent. 143/

Overseas Administration, Federal-
State Relations, and Federal Research

The Commission forwarded three short, unrelated reports to Congress within the format of a single report.

The War and its aftermath had created new and heavy operational
problems abroad for the United States. There were problems associated with military occupation of foreign lands, trust territories,
and economic recovery programs. The Commission, after a brief survey
of the nature and complexity of the problem, chose not to address the
issues directly. Instead, the Commission recommended "that the Congress direct a comprehensive study to be made of the entire problem
of overseas operations and administration." 144/

From the outset there was disagreement among the Commissioners
regarding the issue of whether the subject of Federal-State relations
was within the Commission's mandate. Nonetheless, a task force was
appointed and it submitted a four volume report to the Commission
(unpublished). The full Commission's report and recommendations, in
turn, were "brief and innocuous." 145/ Even this mild report, however, elicited dissents from Vice Chairman Acheson and Commissioner
Forrestal. 146/ The Commission recommended that the functions of
Government be appraised to determine which could be most advanta-
geously operated by the several levels of Government with the pre-
sumption being that the lowest level practicable would be assigned
the function. The Commission recommended "that the grant-in-aid plan
and program be clarified and systematized." And finally, the Commission recommended that "a continuing agency on Federal-State relations
be created . . . ." 147/

With respect to Federal research, the Commission noted that the
President's Scientific Research Board had recently written a report
on the Nation's research efforts and therefore had decided to forego
creating a separate task force or writing an extensive report. The
Commission did call for more overall coordination of research by an
interdepartmental committee and for the establishment of a National
Science Foundation. 148/

DEVELOPING A CONSTITUENCY

Publicity, the Chairman and the Commission believed, would be
the key to whatever success they enjoyed in having their recommenda-

-tions ultimately adopted. While most commissions and committees have to be satisfied with modest media coverage, largely unread reports, and low-visibility meetings, not the Hoover Commission. They sought to co-opt much of the press by providing the type of stories that conformed to the needs of the media and their perception of Government as a bureaucratic mess. Hoover, contrary to conventional wisdom, had a long history of working well with the press and with publicity agents. 149/ Before the Commission had completed its work, most of the major magazines had run feature stories extolling the reorganization effort thereby raising public awareness and expectations.

Under Hoover's guidance, the Committee created its own interest group, the Citizens Committee for the Hoover Report (CCHR). To head the Committee, Hoover selected Robert L. Johnson, President of Temple University in Philadelphia 150/ and an academic entrepreneur who, in the words of his sympathetic biographer, "exemplified the enterprising spirit of the 1920's and 1930's." 151/ Johnson was steeped in the language of the Scientific Management school and had promoted various local civil service reform efforts. Johnson and Hoover worked closely in selecting the 28 member Board of Directors for the CCHR.

The CCHR moved in stages, first with more than 700 prominent citizens listed as supporters including luminaries such as former Vice Presidents Charles Dawes and John Nance Garner, numerous former Cabinet officers, Federal officials, governors and leaders of labor, business, farm, church, education, professional, veterans and women's organizations. 152/ Next, Citizens Committees were formed in 45 States with 300 county and local affiliates. Even allowing for organizational hyperbole, this was an impressive effort. Funding for the Commission came from foundations, corporations, and individuals. The central office prepared vast quantities of materials for distribution and for other national organizations to distribute to their own memberships. 153/ Finally, the Citizens Committee drafted many legislative proposals and submitted them to the relevant committees of Congress.

The principal message of the Citizens Committee, and its tireless leaders, was that savings of billions, the most common figure cited was $4 billion, was possible if all the recommendations of the Commission were adopted. Even Mr. Hoover made this claim. 154/

Claims of savings had been a source of contention throughout the deliberations of the Commission, as well as afterward. Commissioners Acheson and Rowe, for instance, characterized savings estimates contained in the Task Force Report on the Department of Agriculture as sheer "guesswork." In their opinion, the fact that the Commission itself deliberately shied away from publishing comprehensive estimated savings figures did not absolve it from responsibility for figures published by subunits if the Commisison remained silent. "The mere fact that we publish any figure, even if it is

not our own, would indicate to Congress and the public that we have
no reason to quarrel with such a figure. For the reasons above we
think we do have such a quarrel." 155/

Objections to the use of "savings estimates" in no substantial
way reduced their appeal or utility to the Citizens Committee.
Compromise was not considered a virture by the CCHR in this instance.

Management issues were not stressed by the CCHR in their presentation to the public. The CCHR refused even a White House request
that the Commission drum up support for better pay for Government
executives. The Commission's usual tactic was to employ "horror
stories" to erode the people's confidence in how their Government
functions as a preliminary and necessary step for gaining public support for the Commission's report. Typical in this regard was Johnson's remarks before a group of Texas businessmen "that there are
thirty-six machines for every stenographer on the Federal payroll and
it costs the taxpayers $10 to process every Federal purchase, even a
$.50 typewriter ribbon." 156/

The public relations effort, although prone to simplistic inter-
pretions of crude statistics, was nonetheless considered effective.
Herbert Emmerich later observed:

> The public relations of Hoover I was a serious profes-
> sional job, a job which the Brownlow Committee had neglected,
> and which supporters of Hoover II pushed beyond the limits
> of credibility . . . .
> The acceptance by the press and by radio commentators
> of the first Hoover Reports was unprecedented. The printing
> press continued to pour out untold pages of material con-
> cerning them. This material varied from packaged propa-
> ganda promising vast and undocumented saving to the excellent
> appraisals by publicists and the more penetrating analyses
> by scholars in scientific journals. 157/

The relationship between the CCHR and the White House was correct, if not cordial, with both sides seeking to avoid confrontation.
Generally speaking, the White House, and the supporters of a strong
managerial presidency, were pleased that the CCHR had chosen "savings" as their theme because this meant, in their opinion, that most
of the significant aspects of the Hoover Report would be missed by
the press and the public and thereby engender little opposition.

RECORD OF RESULTS

"The record of results," Herbert Emmerich concluded, "achieved
after the Commission submitted its recommendations was extraordinary." 158/ Even before the Commission had submitted its report in

March 1949, however, it had written the Speaker of the House on January 13, to request that Congress renew the President's authority to submit reorganization plans. 159/ Congress passed a Reorganization Act largely along the lines proposed by the President, but provided for a one-House veto of plans rather than requiring a concurrent resolution. The one-House veto provision was inserted as trade-off for Senate agreement to eliminate exemptions of favored agencies from coverage under the Act 160/ and was considered by bill supporters to be a major set-back for the reorganization movement. 161/

A number of major laws were passed, or at least assisted in their passage, by the issuance of the Commission recommendations. Included in this number would be the Reorganization Act of 1949, (63 Stat. 203); Reorganization of the Department of State, (63 Stat. 111); Federal Property and Administrative Services Act (creating the General Services Administration), (63 Stat. 377); National Security Act Amendments of 1949 (63 Stat. 578); Classification Act of 1949 (Federal employees), (63 Stat. 460); and the Budget and Accounting Procedures Act of 1950, (64 Stat. 832). In addition, the creation of the Department of Health, Education and Welfare by Reorganization Plan No. 1 of 1953, was considered a product of the first Hoover Commission. 162/

Although some observers believed that the one-House veto provision in the Reorganization Act preordained failure for many presidential reorganization plans, the results suggest that their prediction missed the mark. More reorganization plans were approved in 1949 and 1950 than ever before or since.

In 1949, President Truman submitted seven reorganization plans to Congress. 163/ The press gave a favorable response to the plans. All the plans were significant in their impact and in previous years would have generated considerable controversy. The Administration, as well as the CCHR, encountered some difficulties, however, as the plans did not provide for any substantial savings. Indeed, Plan No. 1 ran into opposition because it would clearly have expanded the Federal Government's role in the health field. 164/

The remaining six plans became effective although there was considerable controversy over several of them. "Truman could regard congressional treatment of his 1949 plans," William Pemberton concluded, "with a good deal of satisfaction." 165/

In 1950, the President submitted 27 reorganization plans. The plans fell into groups. Plans one through six provided that responsibilities for the performance of all functions within six departments be vested in the secretary of those departments. Previously, the authority to perform functions had been dispersed by Congress. The purpose of these plans was to establish clear lines of responsibility from the President on down through the lowest level of the department.

A second group of plans was submitted to improve the internal
administration of the regulatory agencies. These plans were designed
to enhance the managerial authority of the chairmen. Three plans
were proposed to assist the General Services Administration as the
central service agency. In an attempt to meet the objections of
those opposed to the defeated 1949 reorganization plan to create a
Department of Welfare, Truman submitted a plan to create a new Department of Health, Education and Security, but left the independent
statutory authorities of the Surgeons General and Commissioner of
Education intact.

There was more than a little conflict over some of the plans. A
review of the six plans transferring all statutory authority for programs from agency chiefs to departmental secretaries is instructive
regarding the real issues at stake. One unidentifiable CCHR officer
correctly characterized the executive-congressional debate:

> The President's efforts in reorganization have
> almost entirely been devoted to clarifying lines of
> authority and affixing responsibility. His interest
> in this matter is natural because he is both a politician
> and a management man. The reforms he can put through
> in this field make him more effective as a political
> figure because he can control his own bailiwick and
> also make it easier for him as a manager because he can
> run the operation a lot easier . . . . The opposition
> to these Plans was based upon the desire of the Republi-
> cans and conservative Democrats to prevent this assertion
> of authority so that the agencies concerned would deal
> directly with Congress, and hence, with the coalition
> majority in it. 166/

The role of interest groups should not be ignored. As a general
proposition, they fare best when executive authority is fragmented,
so it is not surprising that they were opposed to many of the plans.
With respect to the regulatory commissions, they generally opposed,
as did many members of Congress, transferring powers to the chairman.
Advocates of the Hoover Commission recommendations found themselves
split in their support of many of the reorganization plans. Overall,
in 1950, the President fared reasonably well in having 22 of his 27
plans approved.

The years 1951 and 1952 were difficult ones for President Truman
in a political sense. His Adminsitration was burdened by the Korean
War and distracted by a number of scandals involving key agencies
including the Bureau of Internal Revenue (BIR). Truman's interest
in reorganization steadily waned as his Administration progressed.

The first Hoover Commission produced many results, including
actions not intended or desired by those who originally sought its
creation. The number of specific recommendations that ultimately
were adopted, either wholly or in part, was considered remarkable.
The CCHR concluded that of the Commission's 273 recommendations to

the President and Congress, 196, or 72 percent, of the recommendations were adopted. 167/

A concentration on the reorganization of departments, agencies
and certain functions, while important, tends to obscure what to many
was the principal achievement of the first Hoover Commission, namely
the enhancement of the presidential office as manager of the Government. Peri Arnold, a Hooverian scholar, observed:

> It was the supreme political accomplishment of the
> first Hoover Commission that it masked the managerial
> Presidency with the older values of administrative ortho-
> doxy and, to a significant degree, undercut the conserva-
> tive and Congressional opposition to the expansive
> executive . . . . In the end, Hoover and his Commis-
> sion provided the bridge over which the . . . . old
> political enemies of Franklin Roosevelt could embrace
> the managerial Presidency. 168/

It should be remembered that the deliberations of the first
Hoover Commission were conducted in the shadow of the 1948 presidential election, an election that President Truman unexpectedly won
and which threatened the existence of the Commission. 169/ Hoover
made accommodations to the re-elected President and his views that
subtly altered the philosophy of the Commission, much to the dismay
of some of its early supporters.

Three factors appear to have contributed substantially to the
perceived and genuine success attributed to the first Hoover Commission. 1) There was a working consensus at the time that the institutional presidency and departmental secretaries should be strengthened
as executive branch managers. 2) The relatively small number of
Federal programs at the time made it possible for a informed group to
comprehend the whole of the Government and its functions. 3) The
selection of Herbert Hoover as chairman of the Commission was fortu-
itous as he was both willing and able to be the group leader.

It should also be recognized that the first Hoover Commission
met at a peculiar moment in American history. "A world that had been
torn by crises through the twentieth century," William Pemberton
observed, "because more confusing and frightening as it entered the
atomic age followed by the Cold War. Reorganization seemed to many
people a way to escape various unnamed terrors." 170/ The expansion
and intrusion of the Federal Government disquieted many. There was a
fear of communism and a feeling that America was not adequately meeting the threat. These factors, and others, led many Americans to
desire active measures; and the Hoover Commission with its promise
of reorganization gave the appearance, if not the reality, of much-
needed action.

60

1/ Harry S. Truman, Memoirs: Years of Decision, v. 1, (Garden City, New York: Doubleday and Company, 1955), p. 12.

2/ The 1945 Reorganization Act, like the 1939 Reorganization Act, required that a concurrent resolution be passed in order for Congress to "veto" a reorganization plan. This procedure gave a tremendous advantage to the President and led, in one instance, to the following situation. Reorganization Plan No. 4 of 1939 (April 11, 1940) provided for miscellaneous organizational changes in the executive branch, one change being the transferrence of the Civil Aeronautics Authority from independent status to the Department of Commerce. This provision generated opposition and the House adopted a resolution of disapproval by a vote of 232 to 153. The Senate, on the other hand, rejected the resolution of disapproval by a vote of 46 to 34. Thus, Reorganization Plan No. 4 became law without the approval of both chambers.

3/ William E. Pemberton, Bureaucratic Politics: Executive Reorganization During the Truman Administration (Columbia, Missouri: University of Missouri Press, 1979), p. 79.

4/ Congressional Record, v. 93, June 26, 1947. pp. 7755-7757.

5/ Congressional Record, v. 93, June 27, 1947. pp. 7969-7970.

6/ Ferrel Heady, "A New Approach to Federal Reorganization," American Political Science Review 41 (December 1947), p. 1120.

It is not entirely correct to state that there was no opposition to the proposal. The Comptroller General, Lindsay Warren, stated his opposition.

"As the head and manager of the executive branch, the President has the initial responsibility for good management, including that for the efficient and economical distribution of the work to be performed by it. I am convinced that the power to reorganize should be in him and that it will serve no useful purpose to investigate and report again in the expectation that this will insure reorganization changes being made. That method has been proved to be unworkable."

Letter from Comptroller General Lindsay Warren to the Chairmen of the House and Senate Committees on Expenditures in the Executive Departments to be found in: Congressional Record, v. 93, June 26, 1947. pp. 7755-7757.

7/ The Declaration of Policy in the Act creating the first Hoover Commission (61 Stat. 246) stated:

SECTION 1. It is hereby declared to be the policy of Congress to promote economy, efficiency, and improved service in the transaction of the public business in the departments, bureaus, agencies, boards, commissions, offices, independent establishments, and instrumentalities of the executive branch of the Government by—
   (1) limiting expenditures to the lowest amount consistent with the efficient performance of essential services, activities, and functions;
   (2) eliminating duplication and overlapping of services, activities, and functions;
   (3) consolidating services, activities, and functions of a similar nature;
   (4) abolishing services, activities, and functions not necessary to the efficient conduct of Government; and
   (5) defining and limiting executive functions, services, and activities.

8/ Frank Gervasi, Big Government: The Meaning and Purpose of the Hoover Report (New York: McGraw-Hill Co., 1949), p. 8.

9/ Heady, "A New Approach to Federal Executive Reorganization," p. 1123.

10/ Emmerich, Federal Organization and Administrative Management, p. 83.

11/ Congress, by joint resolution, extended by sixty days the deadline for the Commission to submit its report. "Not later than seventy days after the Eighty-first Congress is convened and organized, the Commission shall make a report of its findings and recommendations to the Congress." Public Law 80-906 (December 31, 1948).

12/ Compensation varied for members who were from Congress, the executive branch, and from private life. Senators and Representatives received no additional compensation beyond that received from their services as Members of Congress. A member from the executive branch received his regular salary, plus such additional compensation, if any, as was necessary to make his aggregate salary equal to the congressional salary of $12,500. Private members received $50 per diem when engaged in the performance of duties vested in the Commission. In addition, provision was made to reimburse all members for travel, subsistence, and other necessary expenses incurred by them in the performance of Commission duties.

13/   "When the Commission finished its work in 1949 after 18
months of investigation, it had spent about $2 million." U.S.,
Congress, House, Committee on Government Operations, Summary of the
Objectives, Operations, and Results of the Commissions on Organi-
zation of the Executive Branch of the Government (First and Second
Hoover Commissions). Committee print, 88th Cong., 1st sess., 1963.
p. 5.
    This committee print will be cited hereafter as: Congress, House,
Summary of . . . First and Second Hoover Commissions (1963).

14/   Congressman Carter Manasco (D-Ala) lost in his 1948 re-
election bid, but remained a member of the Commission.

15/   Speaker of the House, Joseph W. Martin, recalled his
decision process for selecting Mr. Hoover, "I thought at once of
Hoover, knowing that if a former President became a member, he would
almost automatically be elected chairman." My First Fifty Years in
Politics (New York: McGraw-Hill Book Company, 1960), p. 191.

16/   Although James Forrestal was able to serve throughout the
entire period of the Commission, his attendance and interest became
increasingly sporadic due to a mental breakdown. He died in 1949.

17/   While the press was optimistic about the probable outcome
of the Hoover Commission, there were some pessimistic voices. Writing
in 1947, Ferrel Heady, an assistant to Commissioner Pollock, saw
little hope for positive results from the Commission's efforts:
    "Unfortunately, the revival of interest in a
    comprehensive reorganization movement comes at a time
    when the prospect for success in such an undertaking
    seems, on the surface at least, to be unusually dim.
    Even under the most favorable circumstances, large-
    scale executive reorganization involves formidable dif-
    ficulties. This is a hazardous task, demanding mutual
    confidence and an acceptable working relationship between
    the legislature and the executive. The fatal barrier to
    many efforts at reorganization in the past has been the
    failure to work out a satisfactory modus operandi between
    Congress and the President. The hard fact is that at no
    time since executive reorganization became a matter of
    serious concern in this country has the possibility of
    such cooperative action between Congress and the President
    seemed as remote as it does right now." "A New Approach
    to Federal Executive Reorganization," American Political
    Science Review 41 (December 1947), p. 1118.

18/   The Commission adopted a policy statement on October 20,
1947, which stated, in part, that it was the task of the Commission
to review the necessity and desirability of programs and functions
as well as the organization and management of same.
    "Thus it is clear that the Commission is not con-
    fined to recommending management or structural changes
    which improve the efficiency of performance of the

(continued) executive branch but is clearly directed to
exploring the boundaries of government functions in the
light of their cost, their usefulness, their limitations,
and their curtailment or elimination."

Policy Statement adopted at Commission Meeting on October 20,
1947. Miscellaneous folder, Frederick A. Middlebush Papers. Quoted
from: Pemberton, Bureaucratic Politics: Executive Reorganization
During the Truman Administration, p. 88.

19/ Seidman, Politics, Position and Power, 3d ed., p. 103.

20/ Pemberton, Bureaucratic Politics: Executive Reorganization
During the Truman Administration, pp. 92-93. At least a portion of
the friendship that evolved between Hoover and Truman may be traced
to the fact that both men shared a fate of living in the shadow of
the reputation of Franklin D. Roosevelt.

21/ Arnold, "The First Hoover Commission and the Managerial
Presidency," p. 51. The extent to which "politics" played a role
in the staff selection process should not be surprising to those
who have studied commissions for it is endemic to the commission
concept. Analysis of the extent and type of political considerations
that dominated the thinking of Hoover and his associates was not
possible, however, until the opening of the Hoover Presidential
Library in 1966 made possible the study of private correspondence
between the principals.

22/ The names and titles of individuals on the Commission staff
appear in: U.S., Commission on Organization of the Executive Branch
of the Government, Concluding Report (Washington: U.S. Govt. Print.
Off., 1949), pp. 49-50.

23/ "These titles indicate the existence here of a nucleus
staff designed for and capable of directing the work of the task
forces and facilitating the preparation of the Commission reports.
Actually, the listing is misleading. The executive director [Sidney
Mitchell], a businessman of independent means serving without
compensation, was originally connected with the Commission as an
assistant to the chairman. He was designated as executive director
in the spring of 1948 after most of the task forces were already
set up and functioning. He remained essentially an assistant to
the chairman rather than an executive officer for the full Commission. As later indicated, the actual director, for all practical purposes, was the chairman himself." (Heady, "The Operation
of a Mixed Commission," p. 944.)

24/ Ferrel Heady was one of those who criticized the manner
in which the chairman used the staff.

"Although the central staff contained individuals
of outstanding capacity, the talents of this group were
never fully utilized because of faulty direction of their

64

(continued) activities and a tendency for the Commission and individual members of it to do work
that the staff was fitted to do and could have
done better." (Ibid. p. 944.)

25/ Policy Statement, October 20, 1947.

26/ The task forces, in order of their creation were:
(1) Presidency and Departmental Management; (2) Post Office; (3)
Federal Supply; (4) Transportation; (5) Veterans Affairs; (6) Public Welfare; (7) Fiscal, Budgeting, and Accounting; (8) Federal-
State Relationships; (9) Public Works; (10) Federal Field Offices;
(11) Revolving Funds and Business Enterprises; (12) Lending
Agencies; (13) Federal Personnel Management; (14) Foreign Affairs;
(15) Natural Resources; (16) Regulatory Agencies; (17) Agricultural
Activities; (18) Public Relations Activities; (19) Medical Services;
(20) Indian Affairs; (21) Government Statistical Services; (22) Records Management; (23) National Security Organization; (24) Territories and Dependencies.

27/ Heady, "The Operation of a Mixed Commission," pp. 944-945.
The most complete discussion of the Hoover Commission task force
system is to be found in: Charles Aiken, "Task Force: Methodology,"
Public Administration Review 19 (Autumn 1949): 241-251.

28/ There were only 18 task force reports finally published,
plus one concluding report by the Commission. In some instances,
several task force reports were combined. Two task force reports,
the report on Federal Field Services and Government Information
Services, were not deemed to be of sufficient quality to warrant
their publication, and some supporting documents went unpublished
because of lack of funds.

29/ Aiken, "Task Force: Methodology," p. 245.

30/ Heady, "The Operation of a Mixed Commission," p. 947.

31/ Arnold, "The First Hoover Commission and the Managerial
Presidency," p. 50.

32/ Pemberton, Bureaucratic Politics: Executive Reorganization
During the Truman Years, pp. 85-86. Other students of the first
Hoover Commission who describe Hoover as being the dominant element
on the Commission include: Emmerich, Federal Organization and
Administrative Management, pp. 85-86; Heady, "The Operation of a
Mixed Commission," pp. 947-949; Arnold, "The First Hoover Commission
and the Managerial Presidency," p. 51.

33/ Frank Gervasi, Big Government: The Meaning and Purpose of
the Hoover Commission Report (New York: McGraw-Hill Company, 1949),
p. vii.

34/ Herbert Emmerich, Essays in Federal Reorganization (University, Alabama: University of Alabama Press, 1950), p. 98.

35/ Although Ferrel Heady was willing to concede Hoover some credit for his writing skills, he did not award him high marks for his handling of the Commission's deliberations. Agendas for meetings, for instance, tended to be unannounced or uncertain. Time was frequently expended on subjects not previously announced or on detailed textual reviews. When controversial matters arose, decisions were generally postponed for later consideration. There were complaints about the lack of order, but these complaints were never redressed. "The Operation of a Mixed Commission," p. 950. It should be noted that Heady was, for a time, Assistant to Commissioner James Pollock.

36/ Aiken, "Task Force: Methodology," p. 246.

37/ Summaries of the reports of the first Hoover Commission were published in several contemporary sources, e.g., "Summary of Reports of The Hoover Commission," Public Administration Review 9 (Spring 1949): 73-99. "The Hoover Commission: A Symposium," American Political Science Review 43 (October 1949): 933-1000. Lester B. Orfield, "The Hoover Commission and Federal Executive Reorganization," Temple Law Quarterly 24 (October 1950): 162-221.

38/ The full set of reports appeared in: U.S., Commission on Organization of the Executive Branch of the Government, The Hoover Commission Report (New York: McGraw-Hill Company, 1949). This privately published book will be cited hereafter as the First Hoover Commission Report (McGraw-Hill edition). Dissenting opinions are missing from this one volume edition of the Report.

39/ Ferrel Heady, "The Reports of the Hoover Commission," Review of Politics 11 (July 1949), p. 356.

40/ The five reports in this category are: General Management of the Executive Branch; Office of General Services--Supply Activities; Personnel Management; and Budget and Accounting. The Commission submitted a separate, fifth report to Congress on the Department of the Treasury although the task force report was included as part of the task force report on Fiscal, Budgeting and Accounting Activities of the Federal Government.

41/ Emmerich, Federal Organization and Administrative Management, p. 88.

42/ U.S., Commission on Organization of the Executive Branch of the Government, General Management of the Executive Branch (Washington: U.S. Govt. Print. Off., 1949), p. viii. The reports of the first Hoover Commission will be cited hereafter as: First Commission, Name of Report.

43/ Ibid., pp. 7-8.

66

44/ "The Hoover Commission and many of its collaborators are
Mr. Brownlow's children," according to Herman Finer, "even if Mr.
Hoover did not realize it." "The Hoover Commission Reports,"
Political Science Quarterly 64 (September 1949), p. 412. Also:
Emmerich, Federal Organization and Administrative Management, p. 90.

45/ The Commission's report, General Management of the Executive Branch, according to Harold Seidman, " . . . represents the
most categorical formulation of the orthodox or classical organization doctrine derived largely from business administration and identified with the scientific management movement during the early decades of this century . . . ." Politics, Position, and Power,
3rd ed., pp. 4-5.

46/ First Hoover Commission Report (McGraw-Hill edition), p.
21.

47/ First Commission, General Management of the Executive
Branch, p. 56. The statement that the Commission desired fewer agencies tends to obscure a debate that occurred within political science
circles during the period the first Hoover Commission was meeting.
The Brownlow Committee had sought to incorporate most of the independent agencies into executive departments with the latter category of
organization being limited to twelve in number to facilitate presidential "span of control." A number of political scientists (including James Pollock and John D. Millett, the latter a staff member who
contributed to the task force report on departmental management)
were on record as objecting to the Brownlow Committee's proposal as
too rigid. They generally favored more, medium-sized departments
rather than fewer, larger departments. An augmented Executive Office of the President, in their view, could handle any increased
problems in coordination. Edward Hobbs, Behind the President: A
Study of Executive Office Agencies (Washington: Public Affairs
Press, 1954), pp. 7-8. John D. Millett, "Post-War Trends in Public
Administration in the United States," Journal of Politics 11
(November 1949), p. 746.

48/ Proponents of "Cabinet Government" were dissatisfied with
the Commission and its report. The notion that the "solitary" President ought to be strengthened as the chief manager of the Federal
Government was particularly galling to them. In the words of Herman
Finer:

  "A full cabinet system with collective responsibility
  is the crying need of America—of the nation, of the Congress,
  of the departments, of the civil service, and of the presidency. Only if the responsibility is truly shared among
  fifteen or twenty men, only if the will to govern is put into
  commission, will it be possible to integrate the Government
  of the United States, and secure simultaneously that all
  departments shall be heard, that all departments shall take
  notice, that all personnel shall respect their chief, that
  facts and advice shall not run about free, equal, and wild."

(continued) "The Hoover Commission Reports," Political Science Quarterly 64 (September 1949), p. 417.

49/ First Commission, General Management of the Executive Branch, pp. 17-18.

50/ First Commission Report (McGraw-Hill edition), p. xv. Congress did pass legislation giving the President reorganization authority without agency exemptions, but limited the authority to four years and provided for a legislative veto by a single House. Ferrel Heady, "The Reorganization Act of 1949," Public Administration Review 9 (Summer 1949): 165-174.

51/ First Commission, Budget and Accounting, p. 8.

52/ The Commission recommended that the name of the then Bureau of the Budget be changed to the Office of the Budget, in conformance with the Commission's view that all staff units be designated 'offices.'

53/ First Commission, Budget and Accounting, p. 17.

54/ Ibid., p. 39.

55/ There was a difference of opinion among the Commissioners respecting the proper role of the General Accounting Office (GAO) in the political system. The congressional members generally sought to keep both the accounting and auditing functions in the GAO, a legislative agency. The majority of the remaining Commissioners wanted the functions split with the Treasury Department being made responsible for accounting activities in the executive branch and GAO retaining its auditing responsibilities.
For a discussion of the Hoover Commission recommendations and where they fit in the evolution of the budgetary process up to that time, see Arthur Smithies, The Budgetary Process in the United States (New York: McGraw-Hill Company, 1955), chapter 4.

56/ First Commission, Office of General Services, p. 5. Commissioners Herbert Hoover and Arthur Flemming had recommended in their reservation comments in the report on Budget and Accounting that the statistical and publications units then in the Bureau of the Budget be placed in the proposed Office of General Services.

57/ First Commission, Personnel Management, p. 7. For a discussion of this report, see Lewis B. Sims, "Improving Federal Management Services, Personnel," American Political Science Review 43 (October 1949): 990-993.

58/ Ibid., p. 9.

59/ Ibid., pp. 11-12.

60/ First Commission, Treasury Department, p. 1.

61/ Several reorganization plans submitted to implement Commission recommendations were disapproved by Congress, at least in their initial form. The recommended consolidation of the Bureau of Internal Revenue and Bureau of Customs, for instance, was rejected.

Two plans were effected that altered the organization and operations of the Department. Reorganization Plan No. 26 of 1950 continued the independent status of the Reconstruction Finance Corporation, but replaced the Board of Directors with a single Administrator. The Plan further provided that authorities vested in the heads of the Bureaus of Internal Revenue, Customs, Narcotics, the Mint, of Engraving and Printing, the United States Coast Guard, and the Fiscal and Secret Services be vested in the Treasury Secretary. Only the functions of the Comptroller of the Currency were exempted from this transfer. No provisions were included for the proposed transfer of certain agencies in or out of the Department.

Reorganization plan No. 1 of 1952 repealed the requirement of Senate confirmation for collectors and other revenue officials and brought them under civil service.

62/ Alfred D. Sander, "Truman and the National Security Council: 1945-1947," The Journal of American History 59 (September 1972): 369-388. Paul Y. Hammond, "The National Security Council As a Device for Interdepartmental Coordination: An Interpretation and Appraisal," American Political Science Review 54 (December 1960): 899-910. Demetrios Caraley, The Politics of Military Unification (New York: Columbia University Press, 1966).

63/ U.S., Congress, Senate, Committee on Naval Affairs, Unification of the War and Navy Departments and Postwar Organization for National Security (Report to the Hon. James Forrestal, Secretary of the Navy) Committee print, 79th Cong., 1st sess., 1945.

64/ Hammond, "The National Security Council As a Device for Interdepartmental Coordination," p. 901.

65/ Emmerich, Federal Organization and Administrative Management, pp. 91-92.

66/ Hammond, "The National Security Council As a Device for Interdepartmental Coordination," p. 901.

67/ First Commission, The National Security Organization, p. 6.

68/ Ibid., p. 16.

69/ Ibid., p. 22.

70/ The National Security Act Amendments of 1949 (63 Stat. 203) reconstituted the National Military Establishment into the Department of Defense. It provided for basic changes in the composition of the National Security Council, converted the Army, Navy, and Air Force into military departments without Cabinet status, and vested in the Secretary of Defense complete authority and control over the administration of the new Department. The Act further provided for a performance-type budget calling for coordination of the Department's accounting, auditing, statistical, and fiscal policies, procedures and methods over all appropriations and funds allocated to it. Thus, the Commission enjoyed considerable success in having its recommendations implemented in the defense field.

71/ First Commission, Foreign Affairs, p. 23.

72/ Ibid.

73/ Ibid., p. 27.

74/ Ibid., p. 29.

75/ Ibid., pp. 61-68.

76/ Emmerich, Federal Organization and Administrative Management, p. 92.

77/ First Commission, Department of the Interior, p. 1. Vice Chairman Acheson, and Commissioners Pollock and Rowe submitted separate comments recommending a new Department of Natural Resources. pp. 53-54.

78/ Ibid., p. 15. See dissents of Commissioners McClellan and Manasco, both Members of Congress. pp. 81-89.

79/ Ibid., p. 29. Notwithstanding the relatively dramatic quality of the Commission's recommendation to transfer the Army Corps of Engineers to the Interior Department, it represented a "retreat" from the recommendation of its Task Force on Natural Resources. The task force had recommended that the Department of the Interior be terminated and a new, expanded Department of Natural Resources be created in its stead.
> To this department would be transferred the functions of the Bureau of Reclamation, Geological Survey, Fish and Wildlife Service, Bureau of Mines, Oil and Gas Division, Bureau of Land Management, the Forest Service, National Park Service and related research activities; the water development functions of the Army Engineers and the Federal Power Commission; appropriate research activities in mineral economics from the Department of Commerce; and incidental land-title functions from other departments. First Commission, Task Force Report on Natural Resources [Appendix L], p. 9.

80/ Albeit somewhat dated, the foremost critique of the Army
Corps of Engineers and the divided Federal approach to water resources projects remains: Arthur Maass. Muddy Waters: The Army
Engineers and the Nation's Rivers, (Cambridge: Harvard University
Press, 1951). See also: Arthur Maass, "Congress and Water Resources," American Political Science Review 44 (September 1950):
576-592. For an interesting "up-date" on the Army Corps of Engineers, see: Daniel Maxmanian, and Jeanne Nienaber. Can Organizations Change? Environmental Protection, Citizen Participation,
and the Corps of Engineers (Washington: The Brookings Institution,
1979).

81/ Seidman, Politics, Position, and Power, 3rd ed., pp. 49-50.

82/ First Commission, Task Force, Report on Public Works [Ap-
pendix Q]. Included in the proposed Federal Works Department would be
such disparate agencies as the Coast and Geodetic Survey, Bureau of
Mines, Atomic Energy Commission, Tennessee Valley Authority, Bureau
of Indian Affairs, Fish and Wildlife Service, National Bureau of
Standards, and Commission on Fine Arts, among others.

83/ Ibid., p. 4. The Public Works task force had defended its
proposal for a Board of Impartial Analysis for Engineering and Archi-
tectual Projects in these terms: ". . . It would be worth a great
deal to the country to have a thorough, factual unbiased report by
the seagreen incorruptibles of the engineering profession on all major construction projects, especially if such a report were couched
in plain, ordinary Anglo-Saxon English, understandable to the average
layman. We have therefore recommended, as a most important feature
of the . . . new Department, a board of three experts to be known
as the Board of Impartial Analysis." Ibid., p. 12.

84/ First Commission, Report on the Department of the Interior,
pp. 3-4. Chairman Hoover expressed reservations about the Board as
proposed. He wanted two boards, one for engineering projects and one
for architectural projects. He believed that both boards should be
in the Department of the Interior, not the Executive Office of the
President. "[T]he purpose is to review these projects before they
reach the Office of the Budget and not afterward. This device is
proposed as a brake upon hare-brained projects from the departments
and on the log-rolling of projects in the Congress. To put this
agency in the President's Office is to mobilize both these forces
on the President's door." p. 4.

85/ Ibid., pp. 15-16.

86/ The Commission had further recommended that the Bureau of
Indian Affairs be transferred to the new Department for Social Security, Education, and Indian Affairs; that the Bureau of Land Management (except minerals) be transferred to the Department of Agriculture; and that the responsibility for commerical fisheries be transferred from the Fish and Wildlife Service to the Department of Commerce. On the other hand, the flood control and rivers and harbors

(continued) improvement would be transferred to the Interior Department from the Department of Army, as well as Public Buildings Construction and Community Services from the Federal Works Agency. Ibid., pp. 7-10.

87/ First Commission, Department of Agriculture, p. 3.

88/ When President Truman submitted Reorganization Plan No. 4 of 1950 providing for the transfer of all functions vested in other officers, employees, and agencies of the Department to the Secretary of Agriculture, except the functions conferred on hearing examiners and corporations, Congress balked. In the hearings held by the Senate Committee on Government Operations, eight members of the Commission's Task Force on Agriculture testified in opposition to the Plan. The Committee recommended the disapproval of the Plan.

The majority view was that the reorganization proposal, while stated in seemingly neutral, managerial terms, was really a venture into "matters of substantive policy" which have been established by Congress after many years of study. "It is the opinion of a majority of the Committee that to grant the Secretary the powers contained in this plan would mean that the Congress is abjectly surrendering its legislative authority to the Secretary of Agriculture without indication as to how it will be used and without veto powers over any reorganization effected thereunder."

U.S., Congress, Senate, Committee on Government Operations, Senate Action on Hoover Commission Reports, Committee print, 82d Cong., 2d sess., 1952. p. 35.

89/ First Commission, Department of Agriculture, p. 16.

90/ Ibid., p. 23.

91/ Ibid., p. 26.

92/ Ibid.

93/ First Commission, Veterans' Affairs, p. 3.

94/ Ibid., p. 6.

95/ Ibid., p. 19.

96/ It is interesting to note that at the task force level the "analysis of the structure and work of the Veterans' Administration was delegated to a committee composed of prominent insurance company executives. This committee confined its work to the insurance phases of the Veterans' Administration; but as it was appointed to report on the entire agency it contracted all of the Administration's operations other than insurance to a management firm." Charles Aiken, "Task Force: Methodology," Public Administration Review 9 (Autumn 1949), pp. 245-246.

97/ The Commission recommendations regarding the Veterans'
Administration were considered by the President and several congressional committees. The consensus was that the Commission's recommendations were too broad to be put into effect legislatively and
there was need for a major managerial study. The managerial study
completed in June of 1952 and subsequent changes in VA policies and
organization are attributable in part to the Hoover Commission and
in part to subsequent studies by the management firm and congressional committees.

98/ First Commission, Department of Labor, p. 19.

99/ Vice Chairman Acheson and Commissioners Forrestal and
Manasco dissented from the recommendation to transfer the Selective
Service System to the Department of the Interior. Ibid., pp. 9-10.

100/ First Commission, Social Security--Education--Indian
Affairs, p. 6.

101/ Vice Chairman Acheson, Commissioners Aiken and Rowe dissented from the recommendations to separate health functions from other
welfare activities and recommended the formation of a Department of
Welfare, to include health activities. Ibid., p. 37.

102/ Ibid., p. 5-6.

103/ Ibid., p. 17.

104/ Ibid., p. 63.

105/ Ibid., p. 71.

106/ First Commission, Medical Activities, p. 3.

107/ First Commission, Task Force Report on Federal Medical
Services [Supplement to Appendix O].

108/ First Commission, Medical Activities, p. 2.

109/ Ibid.

110/ Ibid., p. 16.

111/ Ibid., p. 17. Chairman Hoover and Commissioner Manasco
dissented from the majority view and argued that the Board be established "with power to determine the policies of the United Medical
Administration." Support for the idea of a board as policy make represented a break from a long-standing aversion to boards by Hoover.
Hoover reconciled this divergence from his previous position by suggesting that this Board would "amount to an interdepartmental committee to determine policy--this is a long-established practice in our
Government." Ibid., p. 34.

112/ Three task force reports; Revolving Funds [Appendix J];
Water Resources Projects [Appendix K]; and Lending Agencies [Appendix
R] were consulted and became the basis of the report on Federal Business Enterprises.
     Work for the three task forces was contracted out. The firm of
Haskins and Sells, Certified Public Accountants, New York City, wrote
the task force report titled Revolving Funds. A. B. Roberts,
Consulting Engineers, Cleveland, Ohio, wrote the task force report
titled Water Resources Projects. And the firm of Price, Waterhouse
and Company, Certified Public Accountants, New York City, wrote the
task force report titled Lending Agencies.

113/ First Commission, Federal Business Enterprises, pp. 9-10.
     "It is highly significant," Goldberg and Seidman noted, "that
the Hoover Commission, while it disagreed strongly about various
details of corporation operations, unquestionably accepted the
corporation as an appropriate instrument for governmental purposes
. . . ." Sidney D. Goldberg and Harold Seidman, The Government
Corporation: Elements of a Model Charter (Chicago: Public Administration Service, 1953), p. 3.

114/ While the Hoover Commission was meeting, President Truman
laid down the criteria for use of the Government corporation option
in his 1948 Budget Message. The use of the corporate form of organization is normally indicated only when a program:
     1) is predominately of a business nature;
     2) is revenue producing and potentially self-sustaining;
     3) involves a large number of business-type transactions
         with the public;
     4) requires greater flexibility than the customary type
         of appropriations budget ordinarily permits.
     U.S., Congress, House, Document No. 19, 80th Cong., 2d sess.,
1948. pp. M57-M62.

115/ First Commission, Federal Business Enterprises, p. 25.

116/ Ibid., p. 40-41.

117/ Ibid., p. 102.

118/ Harold Seidman offers one opinion on the political significance of the Commission's recommendations on the Farmers Home
Administration.

        Application of 'economy and efficiency' as the
     criteria for government organization can produce serious
     distortions, if political and environmental factors are
     ignored. It led the first Hoover Commission to proceed
     from the indisputable finding that the Farmers Home
     Administration's functions duplicated and overlapped
     those of the Farm Credit Administration and the Agricultural
     Extension Service to the seemingly logical conclusion that
     the Administration ought to be liquidated and its functions

(continued) divided betwen its two competitors. The
conclusion was obviously faulty to anyone in the least
familiar with the histories of the Farm Credit Administration and the Extension Service as creatures of the
American Farm Bureau Federation and the most conservative
elements in the agricultural community. The Farm Bureau
was proud of its role in scuttling the Rural Resettlement
Administration and Farm Security Administration, the immediate predecessors of the FmHA. If there was ever a
case of letting the goat loose in the cabbage patch, this
was it."

(Politics, Position, and Power, 3d ed., pp. 16-17).

119/ First Commission, Federal Business Enterprises, p. 43.

120/ Commissioners Aiken, Pollock and Rowe dissented from this
transfer proposal in the report on the Treasury Department.

121/ First Commission, Federal Business Enterprises, p. 45.

122/ Ibid., p. 60.

123/ In describing the inability of the Commission to reach decisions or frame recommendations with respect to Federal business
enterprises, particularly water resources management, Ferrel Heady
observed:

This report evoked no less than six 'separate
statements' by individual members or groups of members of
the Commission, showing a wide cleavage on many matters.
Several of these statements present different points of
view concerning electric power and irrigation enterprises,
on which the Commission could not muster enough agreement to make any definite recommendations. One attacked
the whole organization approach to this report, objecting
to treating together numerous agencies which happen to
use one or more of the techniques of lending, insuring,
or guaranteeing to achieve markedly different public
purposes. Task force studies relied upon by the majority
are subjected to heavy fire in three of the statements
for a lack of objectivity, over-emphasis on accounting
standards, and failure to appreciate the objectives of the
legislation underlying some of the programs . . . .
The total effect is convincing evidence that on this one
basic set of issues at least the Commission fell apart
at the seams. (Ferrel Heady, "The Reports of the Hoover
Commission," Review of Politics 11 (July 1949), p. 373.

124/ U.S., Congress, Senate, Committee on Government Operations, Senate Action on Hoover Commission Reports, Committee print,
82d Cong., 2d sess., 1952. p. 76.

125/ The task force report on the Post Office was written by Robert Heller and Associates, Management consultants, Cleveland Ohio, and was titled: First Commission, Management Organization and Administration of the Post Office Department [Appendix I].

126/ First Commission, Post Office, p. 3.

127/ Ibid., p. 10.

128/ Ibid., p. 16.

129/ Writing in 1937, the Brownlow Committee stated with respect to the independent regulatory commissions:

> The independent commissions present a serious immediate problem. No administrative reorganization worthy of the name can leave hanging in the air more than a dozen powerful, irresponsible agencies free to determine policy and administer law. Any program to restore our constitutional ideal of a fully coordinated Executive Branch responsible to the President must bring within reach of that responsible control all work done by these independent commissions which is not judicial in nature. That challenge cannot be ignored.

(U.S., President's Committee on Administrative Management, Report With Special Studies (Washington: U.S. Govt. Print. Off., 1937), p. 37.

130/ The Hoover Commission task force assigned to study the regulatory commissions viewed the scope of its assignment as similar to that of the Brownlow Committee. Its research approach, however, emanated from a very different perspective.

> In contrast with the high-level approach of the President's Committee, the Hoover Group sought a worm's eye view of the commissions through an extensive program of research into their workings. A staff of survey officers, one for each of the nine commissions, was assembled. Their general assignment was to determine the effectiveness of the commissions as agencies for carrying on federal regulatory activities.

(C. Herman Pritchett, "The Regulatory Commissions Revisited," American Political Science Review 43 (October 1949), p. 981.

131/ First Commission, Task Force Report on Regulatory Commissions [Appendix N], p. 9.

132/ First Commission, Regulatory Commissions, p. 5.

<u>133/</u> The period in which the first Hoover Commission studied
the regulatory commissions constituted the "high water mark" for
presidential influence over the regulatory commissions. Since 1970
there has been a steady erosion in the President's managerial
authorities over the commmissions. By 1981, a number of commissions
were no longer required to obtain Office of Management and Budget
approval of their budgetary requests or legislative proposals prior
to submittal to Congress. Louis Fisher, <u>The Politics of Shared
Power: Congress and the Executive</u> (Washington: Congressional
Quarterly Press, 1981), chapter 5. U.S., Congress, Senate, Committee on Governmental Affairs, <u>Study on Federal Regulation: Regulatory Organization</u>, v. 5, Committee print, 95th Cong., 1st sess.,
1977, pp. 45-52.

<u>134/</u> <u>First Commission, Regulatory Commissions</u>, p. 14. The
two Commissioners advocating a single transportation regulatory
commission were Brown and Pollock. Their views may be found in:
Ibid., pp. 19-22.

<u>135/</u> A succession of reorganization plans beginning in 1950
gradually implemented the recommendation of the task force that
the President be given authority to designate chairmen of the commissions. At present, most of the chairmen serve at the pleasure
of the President, although upon removal as chairman, the individual
continues to serve as a member of the commission for the remainder
of his term.

<u>136/</u> Pritchett, "The Regulatory Commissions Revisited," p. 986.

<u>137/</u> The Commission's recommendations concerning Federal
Transportation Activities appear in the Commission's Reports on the
Department of Commerce and on Regulatory Commissions. The <u>Task
Force Study on Transportation</u> was filed with the <u>Department of
Commerce Report</u>.

<u>138/</u> <u>First Commission, Department of Commerce</u>, p. 1.

<u>139/</u> Ibid., pp. 3-4.

<u>140/</u> A separate Department of Transportation was established
in 1966 (80 Stat. 931). A sympathetic discussion of the rationale
for this Department may be found in Richard W. Barsness, "The Department of Transportation: Concept and Structure," <u>Western Political
Quarterly</u> 23 (September 1970): 500-513. Although this article is
written in detail with many citations to public reports, the Hoover
Commission is unmentioned.

<u>141/</u> <u>First Commission, Department of Commerce</u>, p. 15.

142/ The administrative history of what is presently called
the Maritime Administration is complex. The origin of the Maritime
Administration can generally be traced to the U.S. Shipping Board
established in 1916. As an agency it was reorganized on numerous
occasions. Reorganization Plan No. 21 of 1950 established the Federal Maritime Board and the Maritime Administration within the Department of Commerce as successor agencies to the U.S. Maritime Commission which was abolished. Reorganization Plan No. 7 of 1961
abolished the Federal Maritime Board and established the Federal
Maritime Commission as an independent agency.
       When the Department of Transportation was created in 1966, the
"Maritime Industry" (including organized labor) was able to resist
considerable pressures by the President to have the Maritime Admin-
istration transferred to the new Department of Transportation. The
Maritime Administration remained in Commerce. In 1981, the Maritime
Industry reversed its position and promoted legislation to have the
Maritime Administration transferred to the Transportation Department.
President Reagan signed the bill (95 Stat. 151) on August 6, 1981.

       143/ The National Advisory Committee for Aeronautics and its
research facilities became the nucleus of the National Aeronautics
and Space Administration when the latter was established in 1958.
Alison Griffith, The National Aeronautics and Space Act: A Study
of the Development of Public Policy (Washington: Public Affairs
Press, 1962).

       144/ First Commission, Overseas Administration, Federal-State
Relations, and Federal Research, p. 17.

       145/ Heady, "The Reports of the Hoover Commission," p. 375.

       146/ Statement of Commissioners Acheson and Forrestal:

              This report seems to us to exceed the jurisdiction of
       a Commission created to make recommendations regarding the
       organization of the Executive Branch. Both the report and
       the recommendations contained in it have little to do with
       the organization or even the functions of the executive
       machinery of the Federal Government. They are concerned
       chiefly with taxation, grants-in-aid, and other matters
       primarily in the realm of legislative policy. As a conse-
       quence, we are unable to join in this report or to express
       any view as to the conclusions of the majority of the Com-
       mission.

       (First Commission, Overseas Administration, Federal-
       State Relations, and Federal Research, p. 25).

       147/ Ibid., pp. 35-37.

       148/ Ibid., p. 50. The National Science Foundation was estab-
lished as an independent agency within the executive branch by statute (64 Stat. 149) in 1950.

149/ Craig Lloyd, Aggressive Introvert: Study of Herbert Hoover and Public Relations Management, 1912-1932 (Columbus: Ohio State University Press, 1973).

150/ Pemberton, Bureaucratic Politics, p. 109.

151/ Richard H. Wissler, Challenge to Action: The Life and Works of Robert L. Johnson. Privately published, 1964. p. ix.

152/ "Temple University President Forms Group to Back U.S. Reform," Christian Science Monitor, March 21, 1949. p. 11.

153/ Letter from Robert L. Johnson to Senator John L. McClellan, May 1, 1950. U.S., Congress, Senate, Committee on Expenditures in the Executive Branch. Hearings on Disapproving Reorganization Plans Nos. 7, 8, 9, and 11 of 1950. 81st Cong., 2d sess., 1950. pp. 137-138.

154/ "How to Save Four Billions a Year: Interview with Herbert Hoover," U.S. News and World Report, June 3, 1949, pp. 24+.

155/ Dissenting Statement of Commissioners Dean Acheson and James Rowe, Jr., on the Report on Department of Agriculture. First Commission, Department of Agriculture, Errata sheet, p. 29.

156/ "Hoover Chief Speaks to Group," Dallas Morning Star, April 1, 1950. Part 3, p. 2.

157/ Emmerich, Federal Organization and Administrative Management, p. 97.

158/ Ibid., p. 95.

159/ U.S., Congress, House, Committee on Expenditures of Executive Departments, Hearings on Reorganization of Government Agencies, 81st Cong., 1st sess., 1949. pp. 7-9.
The Reorganization Act of 1945 had expired on March 1948. The President forwarded a reorganization authority bill on January 17, 1949, which was much broader in scope than the 1945 Act. The Administration's bill contained no termination date, no agency exemptions, eliminated the clause calling for a cost saving of 25 percent, permitted the creation of new executive departments (although no new functions), and required both Houses to approve a resolution (concurrent resolution) before a plan could become effective.

160/ The principal agency under the protective wing of influential Senators was the Army Corps of Engineers. In answer to the question of why the Senators insisted upon their view that a one-House veto be incorporated in the legislation, Arthur Maass observed: "Because the Congressional supporters of the Corps of Engineers announced that they would forego outright exemption for the Corps only if Congress would agree to a one-House veto." Muddy Waters (Cambridge, Massachusetts: Harvard University Press, 1951), p. 116.

161/   Ferrel Heady divined unpleasant consequences resulting
from the shift from a two-House to a one-House veto over reorganization plans. "[T]he real objective in inserting the one-house
veto requirement was not just to get rid of exemptions, but to
stiffen congressional powers of resistance to presidential reorganization plans. The success of this effort in the Senate to shift
from the two-house veto to the one-house veto marks a definite
withdrawal by Congress of effective reorganization powers which it
had been willing to delegate in the 1939 and 1945 acts." "Reorganization Act of 1949," Public Administration Review v. 9 (Summer
1949), p. 174.
     For a discussion of the 1949 Reorganization Act and
subsequent renewals of the President's reorganization authority,
see: Louis Fisher and Ronald C. Moe, "President's Reorganization
Authority: Is It Worth the Cost?" Political Science Quarterly
96 (Summer 1981): 301-318.

162/   Congress, House, Summary of . . . First and Second
Hoover Commissions (1963), pp. 6-7.

163/   President Truman submitted eight reorganization plans to
Congress in 1949. The substance of the eighth plan, however, was incorporated in Public Law 216, 81st Congress (August 10, 1949), which
provided that the reorganization plan not take effect.

164/   Reorganization Plan No. 1 of 1949 deviated from the
Hoover Commission proposal to create an independent United Medical
Administration by keeping the Federal Security Agency's health functions within a new Department of Welfare. Also the plan decreased
the authority of constituent units by placing all the legal authority
to operate programs in the secretary of the new department. Adding
to the controversy was the presidential decision to make the existing
head of the FSA, Oscar Ewing, the first secretary. Ewing, long an
outspoken proponent of a mandatory health insurance program for all
Americans, was a red flag to the organized medical community. The
President decided to stick with Ewing and Reorganization Plan No. 1
even at the risk of defeat. The debate was long and vigorous. On
August 16, the Senate defeated the plan by a vote of 60 to 32 in
favor of a resolution of disapproval. Frank R. Kennedy, "The American Medical Association: Power, Purpose, and Politics in Organized
Medicine," Yale Law Journal 63 (May 1954): 938-1022.

165/   Pemberton, Bureaucratic Politics, p. 123.

166/   As quoted in: Pemberton, Bureaucratic Politics, p. 131.

167/   "The Final Report of the Citizens Committee for the Hoover
Report," Reorganization News. October 1958.
     The Commission framed its recommendations in short, declara-
tive sentences. A typical recommendation read: 'We recommend that
customs receipts now alloted directly to the Department [Agriculture]
be paid into the Treasury and that direct annual appropriations be
made by Congress for specified purposes.' The leanness of language,

(continued) often coupled with considerable specificity, might be
criticized, but it did make it easier to keep a tally on accepted
or rejected recommendations.

168/ Peri Arnold, "The First Hoover Commission and the Managerial Presidency," Journal of Politics 38 (February 1976), pp. 48, 49-50.

169/ "There is no doubt that the Commission's ultimate plan was
to have been keyed to a Republican Administration which everyone, except Truman and the 23,000,000 Americans who voted for him, anticipated in November 1948. The Commission's findings and recommendations for changes in executive organizational structure were to have
been the grand overtune of a new Republican era." Frank Gervasi, Big
Government: The Meaning and Purpose of the Hoover Commission Report
(New York: McGraw-Hill Book Company, 1949), p. 8.

170/ Pemberton, Bureaucratic Politics, p. 111.

3
The Second Hoover Commission

Although President Truman had won an unexpected re-election victory in 1948, his second term was essentially a defensive exercise. His goal became that of protecting the New Deal and Fair Deal programs and agencies and one of his chief weapons was the reorganization authority. 1/ Reorganization became one of the means to strengthen the institutional leadership of existing agencies, and was not used to alter the direction of Government.

It was ironic that some of the original supporters of the first Hoover Commission were disappointed with the results while most of the early critics were pleased. The principal results of the first Commission were that the institutionalized presidency was strengthened as were the managerial authorities of the departmental secretaries and agency chiefs. Both these results appeared to many conservatives, however, as significant steps towards a more, not less, interventionist Government. What they wanted, then, was another "citizens commission," again headed by Hoover, this time to attack "Big Government" at its roots. Robert Johnson, initially, took a leading role and raised $100,000 to sponsor and publish a Temple University Survey of Federal Reorganization. The Survey, begun in October 1952, during the presidential campaign, consisted of contributions from 102 persons many of whom had served in some capacity on the first Hoover Commission. President-elect Dwight Eisenhower was notified that this Survey was underway in December and received a copy in October 1953.

The Temple Survey itself proved unimportant, but the fact that it was being compiled spirred others to action. The movement for a second Hoover Commission gained momentum among the recently ascendent Republican leadership in both chambers.

The newly elected President, although a Republican, did not share this enthusiasm for a new Commission, particularly one outside the presidential orbit. In his diary, Eisenhower provided his impressions of the effort to create a new Comission.

> [F]ormer President Herbert Hoover, with a group of
> others, had lunch with me. We discussed the formation
> of a new governmental commission . . . . Mr. Hoover is
> delighted with the opportunity to get back into the middle
> of this big problem. However, I was a bit nonplussed to
> find that the only individuals he wanted on the commission
> were those whom he knew to share his general convictions—
> convictions that many of our people would consider a trifle
> on the motheaten side. As quickly as I found this out, I
> tried to make my other three appointments from among in-
> dividuals whom I knew to be reasonably liberal or what I
> call middle-of-the-road in their approach to today's
> problems. 2/

Early in the 83d Congress, similar bills were introduced in both
Houses to create a new "citizens commission" to study the executive
branch in a manner similar to that of the first Hoover Commission.
These bills were known as the Ferguson-Brown bills.

The President, as was his style, followed an oblique counterstrategy 3/ to this congressional initiative by creating on his own
authority a President's Advisory Committee on Government Organization
(PACGO), a three member panel headed by Nelson Rockefeller. 4/ He
also requested Congress to create a Commission on Governmental
Functions and Fiscal Resources (later to be known as the Commission
on Intergovernmental Relations or the Kestnbaum Commission after its
chairman, Meyer Kestnbaum). The proposals for a second Hoover Commission and the Kestnbaum Commission were considered at the same time
by Congress resulting in some confusion on the part of Members. The
work of these two Commissions proceeding simultaneously and both
reported to the President and Congress in 1955. 5/ Throughout this
period, the Kestnbaum Commission remained closer to the institutional
presidency than did the second Hoover Commission and Mr. Kestnbaum
became an adviser to Mr. Eisenhower on management and organizational
matters.

As with the legislation creating the first Hoover Commission
in 1947, floor debate on the proposed new Commission was perfunctory
with no evident opposition. Both Houses unanimously approved the
establishment of the Commission and the President signed the bill
on July 10, 1953 (P.L. 108; 67 Stat. 184).

The Commission was given the authority to appoint and fix compensation of such personnel as it deemed advisable, "without regard
to the provisions of the civil service laws and the Classification
Act of 1949, as amended." 6/ This latter exemption represented a
change from the original 1947 legislation creating the first Commission as did the provision permitting the hiring of private consultants.

THE COMMISSION

The Commission consisted of 12 members; four appointed by the President, two from the executive branch and two from private life; four appointed by the President pro tempore of the Senate, two from the Senate and two from private life; and four appointed by the Speaker of the House of Representatives, two from the House and two from private life. Unlike the law creating the first Commission, the legislation creating what rapidly became known as the second Hoover Commission did not impose a partisan parity requirement upon the selection process. The Commission at its initial meeting, held in the White House with President Eisenhower in attendance, unanimously elected Herbert Hoover as chairman although the Commission did not elect a vice chairman, as authorized in the legislation.

Membership on the first Commission in 1947 was required to be bipartisan, half the members Democratic and half Republican. This requirement was missing from the legislation creating the second Hoover Commission. Although the enabling act of the second Commission did not limit the appointing authorities in the selection of Commissioners, the Report of the Senate Committee on Government Operations suggested that "appointing authorities might well consider the inclusion of former members of the Commission who may be available, so as to give the new Commission the full benefit of their experience and qualifications." 7/ The Commission that resulted consisted of seven Republicans and five Democrats.

The members of the second Hoover Commission:

1. Herbert, Hoover, Chairman. (Republican)

2. Homer Ferguson, U.S. Senator from Michigan (resigned April 4, 1955; succeeded by Styles Bridges, U.S. Senator from New Hampshire). (Republican)

3. Clarence J. Brown, Member of the House of Representatives from Ohio. (Republican)

4. Herbert Brownell, Jr., Attorney General of the United States. (Republican)

5. James A. Farley, business executive, former Postmaster General of the United States. (Democrat)

6. Arthur S. Flemming, Director, Office of Defense Mobilization. (Republican)

7. Chet Holifield, Member of the House of Representatives from California. (Democrat)

8. Solomon C. Hollister, Dean of College of Engineering, Cornell University. (Republican)

9. Joseph P. Kennedy, financier, former Ambassador to Great Britain. (Democrat)

10. John L. McClellan, U.S. Senator from Arkansas. (Democrat)

11. Sidney A. Mitchell, investment banker, formerly Executive Director of the first Hoover Commission, and official in the Departments of State and Navy. (Republican)

12. Robert G. Storey, Dean of the School of Law, Southern Methodist University. (Democrat)

Five members of the second Hoover Commission had previously served on the first Hoover Commission; namely, Chairman Hoover, Congressman Brown, Senator McClellan, Mr. Kennedy and Mr. Flemming. One member of the new Commission, Sidney Mitchell, had been Executive Director of the first Hoover Commission. In addition, the Executive Secretary of the Commission, Francis Brassor, had also been the Executive Secretary of the first Commission. Sidney Mitchell, in addition to being a member of the Commission also served the Commission in a full-time capacity and acted as the Chairman's deputy. Certain staff personnel had held similar positions with the earlier Commission. All in all, there was a substantial amount of continuity between the Commissions.

The issues that provoked controversy did not divide the Commission members along partisan lines so much as along ideological lines. Roughly speaking, the liberal position was in favor of a larger role for the Federal Government, the conservative position favoring a lesser role for Government. In these terms, the membership of the Commission was more conservative than had been the case with the first Commission. Dean Acheson, James K. Pollock, and James Rowe, members of the first Commission who had been promoted a larger governmental role, were absent from the Commission. The liberal position on the second Commission was assumed by Commissioners Holifield, Farley, both Democrats, and Brownell and Fleming, both Republicans. 8/

Mandate

The sponsors of the legislation had been forthright in stating their intentions for the Commission. Senator Homer Ferguson pointed out in his testimony before a Senator Committee:

The most important difference between this bill and the
Hoover Commission statute [1949] is found in the declaration-
of-policy section. These paragraphs are intended to make
certain that this Commission has full power to look into the
activities of the Federal Government from the standpoint of
policy and to inquire, 'Should the Government be performing
this activity or service, and if so, to what extent?' This
Commission must ask questions of this nature which the
original Hoover Commission did not ask. 9/

Former President Hoover, in discussing the first Commission before a House Committee, commented that the earlier Commission "was
unable to report on policy questions." 10/ The new Commission, in
Hoover's view, was under no such constraints. The Commission could
make recommendations on policy issues as well as administrative issues. The decision to give this Commission a broad mandate to study
policies as well as organization and to offer recommendations on both
was considered pivotal. The underlying premise, or as Hoover called
it, the "philosophy of the Commission," was clearly that the Federal
Government had grown too large and interventionist and that this
trend needed to be reversed.

In furtherance of this mandate to offer opinions on what the
Government ought not be doing, the Commission was directed: "The Final Report of the Commission may propose such constitutional amendments, legislative enactments and administrative actions as in its
judgment are necessary to carry out its recommendations." [Sec. 9(b)]

Although a broad interpretation of the Commission's mandate was
held by the Commission's sponsors and Mr. Hoover, it is not surprising that this interpretation generated controversy. One member of
the Commission, Representative Chet Holifield, first as ranking minority member and then chairman of the House Government Operations
Committee, later disputed the idea that the Commission had been given
a mandate to delve into policy matters. In a separate statement to
the Final Report of the Commission in 1955, Holifield argued:

A plain reading of the enabling statute lends little
support, in my judgment, to the contention that this Commission had a positive mandate to examine and make recommendations in policy matters . . . . But granting,
for the sake of argument, that the Commission had a policy
mandate, common sense would dictate that it should be
discharged within carefully circumscribed limits. Otherwise the Commission is placed in the anomalous role of
sitting in judgment on the wisdom of any and all enactments
of the legislature which created it. 11/

Holifield continued by questioning the wisdom of the whole concept of creating unelected commissions to second-guess, in effect, e-
lected assemblies. He concluded that the creation of policy-oriented

commissions, such as the second Hoover Commission, was "an unwise
departure from representative government." The "mandate battle"
continued throughout the life of the Commission and indeed remains
as issue confronting all "citizens commission" proposals to this day.

Commission Staff

The central staff of the second Hoover Commission was small and
highly supportive of the Chairman; they generally viewed their task
as ministerial and clerical. The great bulk of the investigation,
research and writing was to be left to the staffs of the several task
forces and the consulting organizations. In most respects, the central staff was similar to that of the first Commission except that
they were not responsible for developing a set of summary reports in
a common format for submittance to Congress. 12/

The initial Executive Director of the Commission, John Hollis-
ter, was replaced in 1955 by W. Hallam Tuck. According to the Final
Report of the Commission, the central staff consisted of 76 persons.
This included (1) twelve Commissioner's assistants; (2) the Executive
Director and his deputy; (3) a four member Office of the Executive
Secretary (headed by Francis Brassor, who had been the Executive
Secretary of the first Hoover Commission); a four member Office of
the Director of Research (headed by Harold Metz); a seven member Of-
fice of Editorial Director (headed by Neil MacNeil); a two member
Office of Legislative Drafting (headed by Henry Wood); and a 46 per-
son administrative and clerical staff.

In a manner similar to that of the first Commission, the central
staff consisted for the most part of persons with close associations
and loyalty to Mr. Hoover. The central staff did not coordinate the
activities of the task force staffs.

Task Forces

Like the first Commission, the second Commission decided at its
first meeting to distribute its research load among task forces.
Various functions and processes were assigned to what became nineteen task forces, plus three subcommittees. 13/ These task forces
varied considerably in size, from five members on the Paperwork
Management task force to 26 members on the Water Resources and Power
task force. Similarly, the size of the staffs working for task
forces varied. There is some disagreement as to the total number
of persons involved with the Commission. MacNeil and Metz estimated that "close to 200 men served on the Task Forces and Committees of the Commission" 14/ while James Fesler states that the Commission "was assisted by 513 persons at the peak of employment." 15/

Regardless of which figure is accepted, there were a large number of persons involved, particularly if agency detailees, consultants, and Bureau of the Budget personnel are included.

Both the membership of the task forces and their staffs were heavily weighted in favor of the business community. Supporters of this selection process were lavish in their praise. "The roster of the Commission's investigators," noted MacNeil and Metz, "made one of the most distinguished groups ever assembled for one job in the United States." 16/ Critics, on the other hand, such as Herbert Emmerich, were distressed at the paucity of academically oriented personnel on the task forces and their staffs. 17/

Some task forces, e.g., Water Resources and Power, indulged in the purest form of policy advocacy, while others, e.g., Defense Paperwork Management, were largely satisfied with reciting statistics laced with occasional "horror stories." Since one of the "selling points" for the citizens commission concept was that it would utilize teams of "experts," the individual Commission members found it difficult to challenge or second-guess their chosen experts. Also, many of the task force reports were exceedingly technical thereby encouraging the Commission members "to leave well-enough alone." On the other hand, even subject-area experts like to have their opinions range afield. William Divine describes the problem:

> One of the commission's greatest problems was to harness this group of experts in a wide variety of subject-matter fields. For if the commission was to fulfill its broad charter, it must make certain that the expert's advice is confined to the fields on which he is qualified as an expert. To individual commission members serving on a part-time basis, faced with deadlines, and confronted with imposing task force reports from skilled technicians, this problem must have at times seemed insurmountable. 18/

The problems encountered by the Commission with its task forces and with organizing its own deliberations may be laid, in large measure, to the fact that there was no dominant organizational perspective guiding their work. Task forces each went their own way and wrote reports based on their own set of assumptions and facts. Recommendations in some instances were for the consolidation of functions in one agency while in other instances the task force would recommend the dispersal of a function among agencies. Indeed, it is difficult to discern any substantial supervision or coordination over the task forces, committees, staff, or consultants by the Commission.

The full Commission met for the first time on September 29, 1953. Much of the work of the Commission during its first meetings was to determine what task forces ought to be established and who should be named chairman of these units. The task force concept was particularly suited to Mr. Hoover's temperament and work style. "He devised the Task Force method of study," according to MacNeil and Metz, "and it proved both effective and economical. It makes it possible for him to obtain the services of men of great ability and unusual talent to serve the Commission for just the time needed to do a study in a given area. It also permitted the Commission to function with a minimum of staff." 19/

MacNeil and Metz describe what they believed was the method of operation for the task forces.

> The Task Forces had a completely free hand from the
> Hoover Commission. Each was simply instructed to find
> the facts and make such recommendations as it believed
> were required in the light of the facts. Never was one
> told what to find or what to recommend. Neither was one
> ever told what not to investigate . . . .

> After the Task Force had finally gathered and digested
> its material and decided on its recommendations, it drafted
> its report to the Commission. Again it had a free hand.
> It wrote its report as it felt it should be written, made
> its own choice of language, and put into the report what
> it wanted to have there. 20/

While this view expressed by MacNeil and Metz is rather ideal-ized, it is correct in assigning a high degree of autonomy to each of the task forces. The task force staffs did not conduct much original research, rather they generally relied on available reports and re-sponses provided by agencies. The agencies were responsive, as was the Bureau of the Budget, and the Commission never had to subpoena a document. Only one task force, Water Resources and Power, chose to hold public hearings.

Many of the task forces broke down into subcommittees. At the appropriate point, the task force would be assembled and agree upon its recommendations to the full Commission. It is interesting to note that members of the Commission did not participate in the task force process, except for Chairman Hoover who occasionally appeared to give encouragement and answer questions.

The task force concept, particularly when accompanied by a high degree of autonomy from the parent Commission, was subject to criti-cism. Fesler concluded that the Commission seemed "quite confused about its role, the role of the task forces, and the relation between the two." 21/ Fesler cited examples where it is not clear whether the recommendations forwarded to Congress are those of the Commission members or of the particular task force. There were instances where Commission members were actually opposed to task force recommenda-tions but signed the report nonetheless on the grounds that Congress ought to have before it the task force recommendations.

Method of Operation

Once the task force reports were received, the Chairman typically appointed three Commissioners as a committee to study the report and draft a working paper for full Commission consideration. The draft would be circulated among the members and staff for comment. The working paper generally omitted or modified a number of task force recommendations. 22/

The deliberative process followed by the Commission was limited, for the most part, to the working papers placed in front of the members. Much time was spent on textual questions with little time spent on discussing the assumptions underlying the recommendations or the possible impact of the recommendations upon the administrative system as a whole. "When the Commission did act as a body on the reports," said MacNeil and Metz, "it took them up recommendation by recommendation, approving or modifying each before it moved to the next." 23/ The process was sequential rather than comprehensive. There was no distinction made between major and minor recommendations nor were recommendations integrated into a single report.

After the Commission had voted on the recommendations and accepted the textual presentation, the three member committee would meet again and incorporate final changes before sending the report to the Government printer. Dissents and explanatory statements were included in the reports although they were downplayed in deference to the majority rule principle and were not included in the privately published summary account of the Commission study. 24/ The reports, when printed, were forwarded individually to the President of the Senate and the Speaker of the House of Representatives. The legislation creating the Commission had not provided for the President to receive the reports.

A short Final Report to the Congress was submitted in June 1955 explaining the work of the Commission, listing "possible savings in Federal expenditures" expected from adoption of the recommendations, 25/ and separate statements from Commissioners. With respect to the latter point, Commissioner Chet Holifield submitted a strong statement of reservation about the work of the Commission in general. 26/

In the enabling legislation for the second Commission, the Commission was authorized to propose legislation to carry out its recommendations. A legislative drafting service (2 staff members) was created and wrote some 42 draft bills, but the Commission subsequently retreated from the implication of this activity when it stated in its Final Report:

> It should be clearly understood that the Commission has not considered, approved, or adopted any specific draft legislation in connection with any of its reports nor can

any of the draft legislation submitted be considered as official interpretation or specification of what the Commission means in any of its recommendations. 27/

The second Hoover Commission was granted appropriations totaling
$2,848,534. It expended $2,768,562 and returned $83,527 to the
Treasury. 28/ The Commission ceased functioning on June 30, 1955.

REPORTS

Twenty Commission reports, including the Final Report, were submitted to Congress over a several month period. The reports did not
fall into systematic categories with respect to subject matter. 29/
There was an emphasis, however, on functions and managerial problems
that cut-across the departments and agencies.

Unlike the first Commission, where an administrative model was
offered in the first report submitted to Congress, the second Commission simply examined the several task force reports as they were received, wrote a report of its own and submitted them individually to
Congress. Little philosophical conformity was enforced. Indeed,
there were instances where the recommendations of the second Commission ran counter to the philosophical thrust of the first Commission.

The reports were of widely varying importance and quality. Several reports represented major efforts and proposed substantial
changes. Included in the category of major Commission reports were
the reports on Personnel and Civil Service; Budget and Accounting;
Legal Services and Procedure; Business Enterprises; Lending Agencies,
and Water Resources and Power. The remaining reports tended to cover
subjects of minor contemporary interest or the Commission's recommendations were for minimal changes in agency structure and operations.

The twenty reports of the second Commission contained some 314
numbered recommendations. By 1958, the Citizens Committee reported
that 200 1/2 of the recommendations had been fully or partially
implemented for a "success" rate 63.9 percent. 30/ Assigning full or
partial implementation rates, however, is not an exact science so
that what follows is more narrative than numerical in format.

Personnel and Civil Service Report

"The greatest contribution of the second Hoover Commission to
departmental management," William Divine opined, "is in its report on
Personnel and Civil Service." 31/ The Commission report to Congress
offered some 19 recommendations. While the basic Federal workforce

was evaluated as functioning well, the Commission concluded the management structure of the Federal workforce was in need of improvement.

Three objectives appeared to shape the direction of the Commission's recommendations. First, the Commission sought to achieve a "workable balance" between the roles and responsibilities of the political, or noncareer, executives and the career executives. Second, there was a belief that superior career managers ought to have separate status and career patterns. And third, that the civil service laws ought to be altered so as to improve the appointment, promotion, and removal processes.

The Commission recommended that additional noncareer executive positions be created so that career administrators could "be relieved by the noncareer executives of responsibilities for advocacy or defense of policies and programs . . . kept out of direct participation in political controversies." 32/ One objective of the Commission was to make clearer the distinctions between noncareer and career executives. Such distinctions, it was hoped, would "neutralize" the career administrator.

The Commission was concerned that both the noncareer and career management positions were underpaid and therefore not attractive to the most competent executives. The Commission, therefore, recommended significantly higher pay for executives and a review of conflict of interest laws to determine if they tended to discourage otherwise competent persons from entering into the Federal service. As part of the effort to upgrade management, the Commission recommended the establishement of a Senior Civil Service.

> We recommend that Congress authorize and the President establish a Senior Civil Service composed of highly qualified, politically neutral career administrators nominated by their employing agencies and appointed after careful selection by a bipartisan Senior Civil Service Board with the consent of the President to serve in positions agreed upon by the Board and the employing agencies. Such senior civil servants should have status, rank, and salary vested in them as individuals so that they may be employed in a flexible manner in career positions throughout the Federal service. 33/

The creation of a specially trained, senior executive corps of between 1500 and 3000 executives was an idea that had been suggested from time to time. In this instance, the Commission's recommendation initiated a debate within the public administration community by raising fundamental questions about the proper status and role for administrative leadership of the public sector in a democracy.

It was widely perceived at the time, although the evidence was never fully persuasive, that the professional civil service of western European countries, particularly Great Britain, was superior to that of the United States. In those countries there was, and remains today, a well-defined, largely autonomous career adminis- trative structure. At the top of the civil service there is a cadre of "generalist" administrators. The assumption is that there is a core of administrative subject matter common to all agencies, irrespective of the field of responsibility of the agency. The top civil servants constitute a moving body of managers who have few programmatic ties to the agencies where they are appointed for a short period.

The traditional view in America was that there were two types of executives, political and career. The political executive was clearly short-term and policy oriented. The career executive, on the other hand, tended to be long-term and administratively oriented. Generally, career executives were well-grounded in the programmatic aspects of their agency. Professional and scientific agencies, for instances, were expected to be administered by professional or scientifically oriented career executives. Most promotions were from within the department or agency. Much of the strength of the administrator was derived from his standing in the profession. This system was considered by many Americans to be compatible with the "democratic ethos" and therefore more desirable than an "elite" corps of generalist senior civil servants on the European model.

The Brownlow Committee (1937) and the first Hoover Commission (1949) did not publicly consider the proposal for a Senior Civil Service. The Personnel Task Force of the second Commission not only considered the proposal, but heartily recommended it. A member of the proposed Senior Civil Service would have special status cor- responding to that of general officers in the Army and would be under a special obligation to serve wherever assigned. 34/

The Commission sought to make the career administrator politi- cally neutral. "Senior civil servants should be fully prepared to serve faithfully each administration that takes office. This means that they must avoid such emotional attachment to the policies of any administration that they cannot accept change and work in har- mony with new leaders." 35/ Critics argued that to exhort adminis- trators to avoid emotional attachments to their agency programs is to prescribe sterile and unimaginative leadership.

The Commission report on Personnel and Civil Service generated considerable controversy over the next several years. 36/ Whatever else it may have accomplished, the report forced public administra- tors to ask fundamental questions about leadership in the Federal establishment. 37/ The line between those seeking an administrative system led by a group of specially trained, selected and protected executives and those seeking a leadership system more nearly "re- presentative" of American society was clearly drawn. By and large,

those favoring a Federal executive service based on "free competition," rather then "professional selection," carried the day. Several years later, Herbert Kaufman reflected:

> The plan was never put into effect, partly because
> the high civil servants themselves were uneasy about
> it, and partly because the idea of an elite group was
> not easy to reconcile with American governmental tra-
> ditions. But the fact that it was not immediately
> adopted did not mean that it was dead, the idea would
> be actively, and heatedly discussed for many years,
> yet another manifestation of the deep commitment to the
> belief in neutralization that moved the civil service
> reformers for a generation. 38/

Over the next quarter-century, the idea of creating a senior
executive service periodically resurfaced and enlisted presidential
support. It was not until 1978, however, that the concept became
law. Under prodding from President Jimmy Carter, Congress easily
passed the Civil Service Reform Act (92 Stat. 111; 5 U.S.C. 1101)
which had as one of its main provisions the establishment of a Senior
Executive Service (SES). The SES is based, for the most part, on
concepts underlying the report of the second Hoover Commission and
indeed has many of the features contained in the Commission's
original proposal. 39/

Budget and Accounting

The efforts of the second Hoover Commission to review the budget
and accounting processes for the executive should be understood as
just one episode in the continuing evolution of the executive budgetary system. 40/ The task force and the full Commission were influenced in a direct way by the recommendations and results of the first
Hoover Commission. In 1949, the first Commission had recommended
what they termed a "performance budget." Performance budgets would
be based on functions, activities, and projects rather than line-
item appropriations. By the time the second Commission met, most
agencies were using performance budgets.

The second Commission was generally pleased with the progress
being made in the budgetary field, particularly with the decrease
in the number of budget appropriations items from some 2000 in 1941
to about 375 in 1955. 41/ The shift toward lump-sum appropriations
and the use of a broader classification system permitted more flexibility by administrators in how the funds were finally allocated.
It had also resulted in congressional committees insisting on prior
approval procedures for "reprogramming" of funds. 42/

The Commission recommended that the Bureau of the Budget be "revitalized" and that the Bureau "place in important agencies one or more well-qualified employees whose duties should include continuous year-round review, at the site of the agency, of agency budget preparation and administration and other facets of the Bureau's managerial responsibilities." 43/

Although several recommendations were intended to enhance the Bureau's management capabilities, the bulk of the Commission's interest was in accounting and auditing processes. Indeed, the Commission conceived of the management function as being subordinate to the budget and accounting functions of the Bureau.

While satisfied that progress was being made in the implementation of performance budgeting in the agencies, the Commission believed that this progress was less than optimal because the budget was based on obligational authority and not actual costs. Therefore, the Commission recommended that "the executive budget and congressional appropriations be in terms of estimated annual accrued expenditures, namely, charges for the cost of goods and services estimated to be received." 44/

Accrual and cost accounting would substitute for the obligational authority arrangement then in effect. Instead of giving agencies authorities to obligate monies, over a period of years, they would receive obligational authority only to cover goods and services used during the year. What about long-term programs, such as building a capital ship? Contract authority would be given for the full amount, but Congress would only appropriate what was necessary for that particular year.

The Commission's recommendations, and the theory underlying the recommendations, came under criticism both from within and without the Commission. The thrust of the criticism was that the majority of the Commission, in following the recommendations of the task force, were advocating essentially private accounting methods to the public sector. The applicability of these methods, it was argued, was at best minimal. 45/ Further, critics argued that accrued expenditures would result in appropriating on a piecemeal basis, allowing small downpayments in the initial year rather than confronting Congress with the total cost of the project. 46/

Although Congress instituted various minor steps to clarify the executive budgetary process and generally accepted the annual accrued expenditures concept for agencies, when pressed with respect to applying the concept to specific agencies, Congress demurred. None of the major budget and accounting recommendations were implemented. 47/

One of the more interesting, and embarrassing, results of the Commission's report on budget and accounting was a brouhaha caused by an estimate of "savings" likely to follow from the adoption of the Commission's recommendations. The Commission published as its

own an estimate of its task force that savings of $4 billion was
possible if the recommendations were implemented. 48/ This estimate, and the method by which it was calculated, was subjected to
much criticism and ridicule. 49/

Legal Services and Procedures

The report on Legal Services and Procedures permits us to examine one of the major problems facing the Commission; how to relate
task force reports written by "experts" with a Commission report
written by "generalists." Chairman Hoover had appointed twelve emi-
nent attorneys and jurists to a task force and gave it full rein to
investigate and "make recommendations on any subject in the legal
field." 50/ The task force took this charge seriously and in so doing wrote a report and offered recommendations based on premises
different from those underlying the first Commission reports and most
of the reports of the second Commission.

The Commission found the report of the task force to be technical and heavily weighted toward a legalistic view of government administration. Like other instances where the Commission was faced
with task force reports written by "experts," the Commission felt
its options were limited. It could not reject the report outright.
The Commission finally submitted a Legal Services and Procedures
report to Congress, based largely on concepts contained in the task
force report, although the report never received majority blessing
from the Commission. In the message accompanying the report, the
Commission tried to place distance between itself and the report,
thereby indirectly announcing its lukewarm support if not opposition,
but laconically noting that Congress ought to have the advantage
of a report written by experts. Commenting on this problem,
William Divine noted:

> [W]hat is the Commission to do with an extremely
> technical report on Legal Services and Procedures, pre-
> pared by an eminent group of lawyers, law professors,
> and jurists? The natural inclination is to leave well-
> enough alone and not be disposed to question the
> technical judgment of the experts. Yet this report
> has serious implications for the civil service system,
> the chain of command within the executive branch, the
> efficient operation of regulatory agencies, and other
> nonlegal problems. 51/

The report called for the enhancement of the Department of Justice with this Department being "given the authority to coordinate
all executive branch legal services." 52/ In the report forwarded
to Congress, there were recommendations that a legal career service
be created apart from the civil service system, a separate recruitment and salary schedule be introduced, and that the Administrative

Procedure Act be amended to extend judicial type proceedings to more agencies. 53/

The assumption underlying the report was that attorneys are a profession which should be exempted from supervision by agency executives, either political or career. Not surprisingly, the report was attacked and referred to as the "lawyers' full-employment act." The recommendations unquestionably flew in the face of the first Commission's administrative doctrine of a strong departmental and agency leadership with direct lines of accountability to all internal units. 54/

Commissioner Holifield, in his detailed dissent, criticized the various proposals to give the Attorney General administrative control over the lawyers in the agencies. "Recommendations of this sort assume that legal services are a homogeneous activity which can be segregated from department and agency functions and supervised by an outside legal authority (the Attorney General)." 55/

Congress proved unsympathetic to the Commission's report and never accepted the recommendation that a legal career service for civilian attorneys be created separate and distinct from the regular civil service and under the jurisdiction of the Department of Justice. Although later years would see increases in the types of administrative decisions assigned to the courts or subject to judicial-type proceedings, few such decisions can be traced directly to the report of the second Hoover Commission.

Business Enterprises

The Commission largely shared the business community's view of the Federal Government. Most business leaders believed that the Federal Government had encroached unnecessarily upon the private sector and that the "inefficient" Government could be improved if it followed more closely the organizational and managerial model of the private sector.

In its report, Business Organization of the Department of Defense, the Commission, for instance, recommended that there be created a "separate civilian-managed agency, reporting to the Secretary of Defense, to administer common supply and service activities" of the military branches. 56/ This agency would "serve all the departments equally in purchasing, inventory control, and distribution to the end of the wholesale pipeline." The military, not surprisingly, opposed this idea.

The Commission suggested changes in real and personal property management procedures for the defense and civilian agencies, 57/

and ways and means to improve "paperwork management," particularly
as it applied to requirements placed upon the business community. 58/
"The emphasis throughout," according to Herbert Emmerich, "was on
divestiture of business operations and on modern business management
and methods under civilian heads of activities retained." 59/

In its report titled Business Enterprises, the Commission began
its analysis with a statement of its working assumptions.

Our economic system is based on private enterprise
regulated where necessary to prevent monopoly and to
provide for freedom of competition.
The genius of the private enterprise system is
that it generates initiative, ingenuity, inventiveness,
and unparalleled productivity. With the normal rigidities
that are a part of Government, obviously, the same forces
that produce excellent results in private industry do not
develop to the same degree in Government business enterprises. 60/

The Federal Government had become involved in a number of business-type enterprises to meet economic emergencies and the requirements of war. In the opinion of the Commission, many of these business enterprises had outlived their purpose and had become subsidized
activities in unfair competition with elements in the private sector.
"The continuance of such activities by the Government must be made
subject to justification; occasionally this can be done, but the burden of proof in all instances must be on the Government." 61/

The bulk of the separate industrial or commercial type facilities were owned by the Department of Defense. The Commission counted
no fewer than 2,500 such facilities, e.g., bakeries, cement mixing
plants. A number of justifications were cited for these facilities,
such as geographic isolation of a base or maintenance of morale. But
the Commission determined that too often these justifications were
pretexts. Commissary stores and post exchanges were singled out for
criticism.

With respect to business enterprises in the civilian agencies,
the conclusions were mixed. For instance, the Commission found the
Department of Justice conducted two business enterprises, neither of
which could be eliminated. One of the enterprises was the Federal
Prison Industries, Inc. This Government corporation provided work
for many Federal prisoners to make products to sell to the Government, mostly to the armed services.

The Commission offered a number of specific recommendations,
e.g., that the Alaska Railroad, under the Department of the Interior,
be incorporated and its rate structure be patterned along commercial

lines. Special attention was given to the General Services Administration because of its involvement in many service activities. Unlike the situation characteristic of later years, the General Services Administration was praised by the Commission for its performance, particularly in taking the agency out of many competitive
business enterprises. The Commission recommended "that the other
agencies of the Government emulate the General Services Administration contracting for such services, and thus support both private enterprise and economy in the Government." 62/

Both the Administration and Congress proved generally unsympathetic toward proposals to remove commercial type activities, e.g.,
commissaries, from the Defense Department. On the other hand,
Congress was more sympathetic toward proposals to remove the Federal
Government from direct competition with private firms.

Lending Agencies

The Commission's report on lending agencies 63/ is worth discussing apart from the more general analysis given to business enterprises because the Commission raised several basic issues. The
second Commission, in a manner similar to the first Commission, appointed a task force to study Government lending institutions and
they, in turn, contracted the Price Waterhouse Company to conduct a
background study. The guiding philosophy of the task force and the
Commission was that while many of the lending programs might have
merit when considered individually, the sum total of these programs
has tended to distort and depress the private capital market.

In its extensive report on lending agencies, the Commission
noted critically their growth in numbers and the complexity and variety of organizational structure and authority. Most of the agencies
and their programs were discussed individually by the Commission and
rather narrow recommendations were offered. On a more general level,
the Commission recommended that more lending agencies be made subject
to the Government Corporation Control Act. 64/ They also recommended
that more of the lending agencies become "mutualized," meaning that
the beneficiaries of loans, guarantees, or insurance ought to make
proportionate payments to retire capital stock owned by the Government. "Thus . . . great numbers of individuals and firms interested in these problems become stockholders and the management in
practice passes into their hands subject to Federal regulation." 65/

"Mutualization," a Commission objective, was proposed as a way
to create hybrid organizations where the best of the private sector
could be mixed with the best of the public sector system. Mr. Hoover
had long been sympathetic to the notion of joint Government-private
ventures. 66/ Critics argued, on the other hand, that mutualization

really meant the mixing of the worst of both systems. 67/ The pop-
ularity of the mutualization concept, or of mixed-ownership Government enterprises, has ebbed and flowed over the decades. 68/ The
Commission's general encouragement to assigning public lending functions to entities outside the departmental structure ran counter to
the Commission's overall philosophy of departmentalism.

Although the Commission was willing to award some credit to the
work of the lending agencies, the Commission noted, disapprovingly
that there was a tendency on the part of lending agencies to expand
their functions beyond the original mandate. The Reconstruction Finance Corporation was considered by the task force as a classic example of the aggrandizing tendencies of lending agencies. 69/ Many
of the lending programs were actually concealed subsidies for certain
favored groups. Loans were often made without sufficient equity to
insure payments in the event of default. Any finally, in the opinion
of the Commission, departmental lending or guaranteeing programs
often possess a fatal attraction politically.

Forty-eight numbered recommendations respecting lending agencies
were forwarded by the Commission. The Citizen's Commission estimated
that 12 recommendations were implemented and 12 more were partially
implemented. Recommendations that various lending programs, e.g.,
Alaska housing loans, be liquidated were accepted. Other recommendations that challenged strong interest group constituencies, e.g.,
a proposal that the Rural Electrification Administration be reorganized so as to operate on a self-supporting basis, were defeated.

Water Resources and Power

The Commission's report, Water Resources and Power, was issued
after much effort, but proved disappointing to those who had placed
their hopes that such a group of "experts" would have success where
politicians had allegedly failed. It was universally agreed that
too many agencies were involved in making policy and operational
decisions involving water resources. The initial objective of the
Commission was to study this whole field and offer recommendations
to reorganize agencies to eliminate "agency overlap and conflict"
and to insure that lines of accountability were clear.

A large task force was assembled (26 members), then divided into four "task groups" to study particular aspects of the larger water
resources problem. The report was by far the longest; 2 Commission
reports, 3 task force report volumes, and the most costly. Unlike
the full Commission or any of the other task forces, the Task Force
on Water Resources and Power held public hearings in five cities
where representatives of various interests from 30 States appeared
or filed statements.

It is interesting that the Commission decided to study "water development" and not "energy development" or "land use development." The decision to limit the Commission just to water development was apparently based largely on ideological grounds; namely, that the Federal Government, at that time, had intervened more directly in water development than in other areas of natural resources development. 70/ Throughout the period in which the first and second Commissions met, there was a series of major battles between public and private power advocates. The controversies over whether the Tennessee Valley Authority should be given additional funding for projects through regular appropriations and whether the Middle South Utilities (headed by Edgar Dixon) and the Southern Company (headed by Eugene Yates) should be encouraged to contract to provide for power for the Atomic Energy Commission within the TVA territory served as a backdrop to the proceedings of the second Hoover Commission. 71/

The Commission published what it labeled as a national water development policy based on nine prescriptive points. 72/ The key points of this "policy statement" appeared to be that water resources ought to be exploited for "optimum use" and that the responsibility of the Federal Government should be to assume the primary role when projects "because of size or complexity or potential multiple purposes or benefits, are beyond the means or the needs of local or private enterprise." Commissioner Holifield not only disagreed generally with the nine points but argued that, in sum, they did not constitute a policy. 73/

The second Commission, like other Commissions before and after, found it difficult to agree on an "organizing idea" around which agencies might be reorganized and settled. 74/ This difficulty was most apparent in the Commission report on water resources. With respect to water resources, four possible operating concepts were suggested; water, natural resources, drainage basin, and economic development. The decision as to which organizing concept "ought" to be implemented is not amenable to neutral, scientific analysis. The decision is essentially political and will necessarily result in both opportunities and costs.

The first Commission had proposed that the Department of the Interior be given the mission of developing water resources and most public works as well. Natural resources was rejected as an organizing concept when land management was assigned to the Department of Agriculture. Where problems were encountered that cut across departmental jurisdictions, the Commission proposed that interdepartmental committees be created to facilitate coordination and that a presidential board to review individual projects be established. Further, they recommended that advisory committees composed of representatives from Interior, Agriculture, and individual States be named for each drainage area. Congress never acted upon these recommendations.

Between the first and second Commissions, President Truman had named a President's Water Resources Policy Commission (chaired by Morris L. Cooke) that reported to him in December 1950. This Commission accepted natural resources as the appropriate organizing concept and recommended that a Department of Natural Resources be created with broad powers and with a decentralized water development program planned and managed by drainage basin organizations. 75/ The basin, or areal, concept for water resources development received another boost with the report of the Missouri Basin Survey Commission in January 1953.

The truth is that public administrators entertained ambivalent attitudes toward river basin agencies because they usually conflicted with the more general concept of agencies organized to reflect function. The TVA may be pleasant for the administrators who run it because they enjoy a high degree of insulation from political accountability and can develop their own fish and wildlife policies and environmental standards, but if there were thirty TVAs in the country, there would be little left for the national, functionally based agencies to perform. And it was never clear how river basin agencies fit into the traditional Federal structure.

The second Commission, as the above indicates, was not writing on a clean slate. Its recommendations were minor 76/ and constituted a retreat from the views of the first Commission in that they did not call for a shift to the Interior Department of the civil functions of the Corps of Engineers. There was mention of the need for river basin coordination, but the Commission made no recommendation favoring the general creation of river basin agencies. The Commission did recommend, however, that several existing water resources units be incorporated and charge rates likely to make them self-sufficient.

The Commission recommended the creation of a Water Resources Board in the Executive Office of the President. The Board would "be created from among Cabinet members, together with five public members, presided over by a non-Government chairman." The five public members would be "recruited from engineers, economists, and others of recognized abilities."

Proposing another "coordinating agency" in the EOP was bound to raise objections. Indeed, the use of the word "coordinate" suggests something more than an advisory committee. Presumably, this body would have the capacity to make decisions and invoke sanctions upon those resisting "coordination." Yet, the Board would be chaired by a private citizen, not an officer of the United States. Leaving aside the legal problems inherent in such an arrangement, it is probable that the President would find such a Board a political and administrative liability.

The proposal to create a Water Resources Board constituted, in the opinion of one observer, the Commission "throwing its hands up" in the face of a complex problem. 77/

Of the 15 recommendations submitted to Congress, only the first, a prescriptive call for Congress to adopt a general policy toward water development, was accepted by Congress. The remaining specific recommendations, e.g., "that Congress authorize a user charge on inland waterways, except for smaller pleasure craft, sufficient to cover maintenance and operation," were rejected.

Other Reports

The Commission submitted additional reports which were either narrow in scope or particularly associated with the issues of the moment. A brief comment will follow on each of the remaining reports.

In its report on Overseas Economic Operations, the Commission recommended that the operating functions of mutual assistance should be transferred from the new International Cooperation Administration (ICA) to the departments and agencies with the Secretary of State, through the Director of the ICA, retaining "policy control" and relying upon various boards and committees to provide the necessary coordination.

The report then proposed that the Export-Import Bank and the Departments of Treasury, Agriculture, Interior, Commerce, Labor and Health, Education and Welfare, respectively, administer categories of foreign aid. Clearly, the objective of the Commission was to disperse the functions of the newly created ICA. The reasoning appeared to be that since personnel doing similar activities were available in the departments and agencies, why not use them and thereby decrease the number of persons in the Department of State. 78/

The Commission submitted a modest report on Federal Medical Services. It duly noted that there had been considerable growth in Federal medical services since World War II and that there was an excess of hospital services offered in certain metropolitan areas, particularly for present and former military personnel. The Commission called for "regionalization" of the military medical services in metropolitan areas as a practical solution to these excessive services. One military service would be put in charge of all military related hospital facilities in a specified area. A number of Veterans Administration hospitals were recommended for closure. A voluntary contributory program for medical care and hospital insurance through a pool of private health insurance companies were proposed for Federal employees. Finally, the Commission recommended that a Federal Advisory Council on Health be established and located in the Executive Office of the President.

As with the Commission's water resources report, the recommendation to place a part-time committee, composed largely of non-govern-
mental personnel, within the EOP to "advise" the President and coordinate agency policies appeared to some as a way to "pass the buck"
and to insure that certain private groups had access to the President. 79/ The Advisory Council on Health would be given the task of
developing a national health policy. As for placing another unit in
the EOP, Presidents have generally resisted, albeit with limited success, the efforts of interest groups and professional communities,
e.g., physical scientists, to gain permanent institutional status. 80/

The report on Research and Development was short and dealt
principally with the Department of Defense. The brief section on
research and development in civilian agencies consisted almost ex-
clusively of analysis by enumeration. There was a list of agencies
and personnel involved in research and development work. There was
little in the report that could be construed as analysis or evaluation. The sole evaluative comment forthcoming from the Commission
was that of all the research and development activities in the Federal Government, "the most beneficent to mankind has been in medical
and health research." 81/ Despite this, the actual amount of Federal
funds, the Commission averred, devoted to basic medical research was
about $18,000,000 or less than one percent of the total Federal funds
for research. The Commission recommended "that greater Federal support be given to basic and medical research." 82/

RESULTS OF THE SECOND COMMISSION

Supporters of the second Hoover Commission were quick to sing
its praises. "[T]he Hoover Commission met all its goals," according
to MacNeil and Metz. "It made a frontal attack on Big Government and
all that it means, but did not recommend the elimination of any one
activity required for the security or welfare of the American people.
All its recommendations stood firmly on American principles of Government." 83/

The Citizens Committee again maintained a running tally on the
recommendations adopted. By their count, the twenty Commission reports contained 314 numbered recommendations. The Final Report of
the Citizens Committee concluded that of these 314 recommendations,
200 1/2 had been fully or partially accepted, for an acceptance rate
of 63.9 percent. 84/ Note, however, that the CCHR used the term
"accepted" rather than "implemented."

This "success" story was all the more impressive, according to
MacNeil and Metz, because of the sorry state of the Government in
1953, just four years after the first Commission had completed its
work and had enjoyed having a high percentage of its recommendations
implemented.

In almost infinite detail these studies present a documented picture of a sprawling and voracious bureaucracy, of
monumental waste, excesses and extravagances, of red tape,
confusion, and disheartening frustrations, of loose management, regulatory irresponsibilities, and colossal largesse
to special segments of the public, of enormous incompetence
in foreign economic operations, and of hugh appropriations
frequently spent for purposes never intended by the Congress.
It is not a pretty picture no matter how you view it. 85/

By working "exhaustively" the Commission brought forth thirty-
nine reports to Congress, counting Commission and task force reports
separately consisting of over 3,300,000 words. James Fesler face-
tiously noted that since the Commission cost approximately $2,800,000
and the results were 314 recommendations, that came to $9,000 per
recommendation. 86/ Throughout the reports, it was emphasized that
the failings of Government were not the fault of individuals, or even
of specific agencies, but of the system generally.

Citing the number of recomendations accepted, wholly or in part,
is a rather crude measurement of the substantive impact of the Commission because there is no distinction made between major and minor
recommendations or between hortatory pleas and specific organizational or programmatic changes. Also, ascribing credit, or degrees
of credit, to the Commission for a particular legislative or administrative decision may be misleading because of a variety of factors
that may have contributed to the ultimate decision.

These qualifications noted, certain changes may be reasonably
credited to the Commission. The Department of Defense was further
reorganized to reinforce civilian control and to unify combat com-
mands. There was a reduction in the amount of Government competition
with firms in the private sector. Veterans' laws were codified.
And there were a number of specific improvements adopted for the
Federal career service.

The accomplishments of the second Hoover Commission were not
generally accorded high marks, the opinion of MacNeil and Metz notwithstanding. In retrospect, even the number of recommendations
"accepted" appears to have been exaggerated. Comparisons with the
results of the first Commission were particularly unfavorable. In
his assessment of the second Commission, titled "Disappointing Results," Herbert Emmerich concluded:

While it must be acknowledged that Hoover II had a considerable influence on reforms of an operating nature, its
larger effects were disappointing, particularly to its enthu-
siastic sponsors. Four general reasons for its shortcomings
may be cited: (1) its terms of reference were too broad
and ill-defined; (2) its method of work caused it to concentrate on the details of business operations and to ignore
the major purposes of governmental programs; (3) it failed

to enlist the participation of the executive branch in its
studies; and (4) the political timing for rendering its
reports was miscalculated. 87/

The philosophical conservatism of the Administration of Dwight
Eisenhower notwithstanding, the 1950s were years in which Federally
run programs were generally held in high esteem and considered efficient and beneficent. Eisenhower, the astute politician, 88/ saw in
the second Hoover Commission and its reports considerable political
risk and his decision to "downplay" the Commission and appoint additional, presidentially-oriented, advisory groups was deliberate and
largely successful.

When the second Commission was established, both Houses of Congress were under the control of the Republican Party. By the time
the Commission submitted its report over two years later, both Houses
were under Democratic Party control. This, coupled with lukewarm
presidential interest and support, signalled from the outset much
tougher going for the recommendations of the second Commission.

The Democratic leadership in the Congress portrayed the Commission as being dominated by "big business" and committed to "re-
pealing the New Deal." 89/ Eisenhower and the moderate wing of his
party, the Republicans being the minority party in both chambers of
Congress at that time, envisioned a rough time if they chose to make
the Hoover Commission recommendations "their" policies, and decided
to put some distance between the White House and the Commission.

It is much more difficult to evaluate the results of the second
Commission than it is the first Commission. The first Commission
had a distinctive focus and definable results. The results of the
second Commission were both fewer in number and diminished in effect.
Concluding evaluations ran the gamut from the undiluted praise of
MacNeil and Metz to resigned disappointment and finally to boredom.

Resigned disappointment is evident in William Divine's assessment of the impact of the Commission's work, actually both Commissions, upon the career public service.

> Unfortunately, one of the inescapable results of
> the second Hoover Commission, as with the earlier group,
> will be to lower the prestige and morale of the public
> service. In its sincere desire to popularize and pub-
> licize its findings, this commission had again asserted
> that huge savings could be realized from adoption of its
> proposals. Unfortunately, the indirect effect of these
> claimed savings, no matter how fanciful, is to strengthen
> the average citizen's conception of the spendthrift
> bureaucrat. Similarly, the emphasis on gigantic figures,
> such as the handling of 25 billion pieces of paper each
> year, the occupancy of enough room to fill 1,250 Empire
> State buildings, or the filing of enough records to fill
> 7 Pentagons, has a similar effect on the citizenry. 90/

James Fesler came to the conclusion that the reports of the second Commission were largely irrelevant by the time they appeared. While acknowledging that a case may be made that there is always some good to be found in a report, if only as a provocation and stimulus to education, such a reward is hardly sufficient for the promise and effort that was associated with the second Hoover Commission. 91/

In some respects, the mixed reception afforded the reports of the second Commission is reflective of deeper differences among academic disciplines and professional groups. How the Federal Government is organized and managed is not the sole preserve of the public administration community. The organized legal profession, for instance, was able to dominate the Commission's report on Legal Services and Procedures. In this instance, the Commission ended up recommending to Congress that it create a separate civil service system for lawyers, run by the top lawyer, the Attorney General. That such a proposal was viewed critically by the public administration community and other professions should not be surprising.

Accountants, corporation executives, engineers, doctors all have their professional biases and objectives. If given their way, they would organize and manage the Government to reflect the values of their profession. 92/ The administration of public services has also been approached from the perspective of various academic disciplines, e.g., sociology, psychology, and business administration. Various types of systems analysis have been applied to administrative problems. All these disciplines and professions have something to contribute, but there still remains the need for an integrating philosophy. It was once the hope that a scientifically oriented public administration could provide the much sought-after grand theory.

What the second Commission seemed to prove, if nothing else, was that in an open clash between the cannons of administrative orthodoxy and the dominant political values, the latter is likely to triumph. Hoover, personally, had been able to avoid this confrontation in his own mind for many years. "Herbert Hoover's perception of the principles of good administration," according to Peri Arnold, "allowed him to skirt effectively the tension between his political values [anti-statism] and his attraction to the apparent efficacy of the positive state." 93/ This separation was fragile, however, and broke down when the second Commission decided to make overt policy judgments.

THE CITIZENS COMMITTEE REVIVED

The Citizens Committee for the Hoover Report (CCHR), created initially in 1949 to promote public and congressional support for the recommendations of the first Hoover Commission, was revived to perform a similar task for the second Commission. In point of fact, it had never legally gone out of business although its staff had been minimal after 1952.

Robert Johnson, energetic chairman of the CCHR during its first incarnation, was unavailable for a similar appointment 94/ and hence the Committee chose Clarence Francis, formerly President and Chairman of the Board of General Foods Company, as its Chairman.

The task of the Citizens Committee in promoting the recommendations of the second Commission proved more difficult than it had been six years before. The recommendations were more controversial, the President less receptive, and there had been a decided shift in the attitude of the media in favor of the public sector and the Federal Government.

Individual interest groups attacked specific recommendations. Veterans organizations, for example, were particularly incensed at the Commission's recommendations regarding the closing of certain hospitals and changes in the policies of the Administration.

Proponents of a generally expanded public sector portrayed the Commission and its report as "shades of McKinleyism." The thrust of this approach was to suggest that not only was "big government" here to stay, but that it ought to be encouraged to expand into new areas. Typical of comments in this vein was an editorial by the Washington Post on the Water Resources and Power report.

> The Hoover Commission report on water resources and power is unlikely to make much impression on the Administration, Congress or the public. The reason is that the report, despite valid observations and criticism, is so reactionary in its guiding philosophy as to be a wholly unworkable yardstick for modern government. 95/

Supporters of Federal ownership of electrical power facilities were able to bring great pressure to bear, particularly with "leaked" threats that the Commission wanted to dismantle the Tennessee Valley Authority (TVA). 96/ The Commission objected to the "hidden subsidies" represented by the low rates charged by the Federal power plants compared with tax-paying private firms. In effect, critics of the Commission "dared" the Republicans in Congress to support the Commission's position. 97/

While Eisenhower did meet on several occasions with Mr. Hoover and with key members of the Citizens Committee, the White House never put its full political strength behind passage of the Commission's recommendation as a package. The President simply picked and chose from among the recommendations that fit his priorities, a practice much to the annoyment of the Citizens Committee leadership since they were wedded to the implementation of all the recommendations.

The Citizens Committee was a very active interest group. It had two offices, one in New York City and another in Washington. A loose network of regional and State chairmen was created and held together

by newsletters and periodic meetings. The principal means of gaining access to the public was through "house organs" of corporations,
unions, and civic groups. Literally hundreds of organizations reprinted or paraphrased CCHR materials and distributed it to their
membership. Describing their plans for utilizing this extraordinary
alliance of organizations for 1958, the "Climax Year," the Citizens
Committee stated:

> Many national civic, professional, women's, farm,
> trade, and business groups have signified their intention
> of continuing hard work for the Hoover Report in the
> coming months. Among these are the United States Chamber
> of Commerce, the National Association of Life Underwriters,
> the American Institute of Certified Public Accountants,
> the General Federation of Women's Clubs, the United States
> Junior Chamber of Commerce (Jaycees), the National Council
> of Negro Women, the National Retail Goods Association,
> and many others. Working with Citizens Committee head-
> quarters they will keep their state and local affiliates
> informed on developments in the new drive for 'better
> government at a better price.' 98/

Background materials were provided to "affiliated" groups free
of charge along with instructions ("Do's and Don'ts on Preparing
Materials About the Hoover Report"). Some of the suggestions were
remarkably specific and candid. "Mention Senator John McClellan and
former Postmaster General James A. Farley frequently to balance necessarily similar mention of Mr. Hoover." Other instructions were to
concentrate on "horror stories."

> Hammer home the 'eternal verities' of the Task Force
> Reports incessantly. An employee turnover annually of
> over 25 percent . . . 5,000 miles of unnecessary file
> drawers . . . air shipments of dogfood to Okinawa; ping
> pong balls to Berlin . . . 25,000 pounds of cement to
> Bermuda . . . 5 year old hamburgers; and a gallon of
> catsup for each pound . . . an 8 1/2 year supply of
> flashlight batteries . . . 125 years' of gear drives.
> These things are still news to most people—old as they
> seem to us. 99/

Among the Don'ts were: "Do not attribute assertions about dollar savings directly to the Commission." "Avoid attacks on taxation
and 'spending' as such." And "avoid also any terms with political
overtones, such as 'Fair Deal,' 'New Deal,' and so forth."

The Citizens Committee never published the amount of money it
raised or expended. While it waged an extensive publicity campaign
for the time, it was not expensive by 1980s standards and did not
require mass mailings for support. Foundations, corporations, and
individuals gave funds and there was a large amount of donated time
and free facilities available to the Committee.

The Committee provided speakers, filmshows, editorials, reso-
lutions, panels and forums, radio and television "spot" announce-
ments, and the like, to all who requested, and the requesters were
numerous. It is difficult not to conclude from a reading of their
activities that this was one of the most extraordinary efforts to
influence Congress, through intermediary groups and the media, that
has ever been attempted in the United States. It is also interesting
to note how little has ever been written on the Citizens Committee in
scholarly journals. The Citizens Committee issued its final report
in October 1958, and disbanded. 100/

1/ President Truman, in 1949, created his own Advisory Committee on Management (Executive order 10072) to study management problems in the Federal Government from the presidential perspective.
This Committee was also to advise him with respect to recommendations
submitted by the Hoover Commission. The final report of this Committee to the President emphasized the need for a continuing program of
management improvement for all agencies under the guidance of the
Bureau of the Budget's Office of Management and Organization. The
final report is reprinted: "Improvement of Management in the
Federal Government," Public Administration Review 13 (Winter 1953):
38-49.

2/ Robert Ferrell, ed., The Eisenhower Diaries (New York:
W.W. Norton Company, 1981), pp. 247-248.

3/ Fred I. Greenstein, "Eisenhower as an Activist President:
A Look at New Evidence," Political Science Quarterly 94 (Winter
1979-80): 575-600.

4/ The President's Advisory Committee on Government Organization (PACGO) was not an episodic body, like the Commissions, but a
three-member continuing body reporting directly to the President.
Herbert Emmerich gave high marks to PACGO. "When the full record of
PACGO becomes available to administrative analysts and historians, I
predict that this small, close-knit, knowledgeable, continuous, dili-
gent presidential commission will prove to have made more construc-
tive and durable contributions to federal organization and administrative management than was produced by all the massive forays of the
task forces and flying squadrons of the Hoover Commission put together." Federal Organization and Administrative Management, p. 176.

5/ The report of the 25 member Commission on Intergovernmental
Relations was submitted to the President for transmittal to Congress
in June 1955. This report consisted of 16 studies. U.S., Commission
on Intergovernmental Relations, Report to the President (Washington:
U.S. Govt. Print. Off., 1955). For background on this Commission,
see: William, Anderson, "The Commission on Intergovernmental Relations and the United States Federal System," Journal of Politics 18
(May 1956): 211-231.

6/ When the law establishing the first Hoover Commission was
enacted, there was no provision for exempting members or employees
from conflict-of-interest statutes, Chairman Hoover subsequently requested Congress to amend the statute to provide for such exemption,
which Congress passed (62 Stat. 1292). The conflict of interest
exemption was included in the legislation creating the second Hoover
Commission.

7/ U.S., Congress, Senate, Committee on Government Operations,
Commission on Organization of the Executive Branch of the Government,
S. Rept. 216, 83d Cong., 1st sess., 1953. p. 6

8/ James W. Fesler, "Administrative Literature and the Second
Hoover Commission Reports," American Political Science Review 51
(March 1957), p. 149.

9/ U.S., Congress, Senate, Committee on Government Operations,
Establishment of Commission on Organization of the Executive Branch
of the Government, S. Rept. 216, 83d Cong., 1st sess., 1953. p. 4.

10/ U.S., Congress, House, Committee on Government Operations,
Commission on Organization of the Executive Branch of the Government,
H. Rept. 505, 83d Cong., 1st sess., 1953. p. 3.

11/ U.S., Commission on Organization of the Executive Branch
of the Government, Final Report to Congress (Washington: U.S.
Govt. Print. Off., 1955), pp. 27-28. This Report hereafter will
be cited as: Second Commission, Final Report. Similarly, where
specific Reports of the Second Commission are cited, the citation
will read: Second Commission, Name of the Report.

12/ It is not entirely correct to state that no summary account
of the Commission's work was assembled by the central staff. Such
a study was compiled but was written as a private venture by the
Editorial Director, Neil MacNeil, and the Research Director, Harold
W. Metz. The volume, The Hoover Report, 1953-1955: What It Means to
You as Citizen and Taxpayer, was published by the Macmillan Company
in 1956. This book, while highly sympathetic and largely self-
serving, will nonetheless be cited often in subsequent sections because it does provide a useful summary account of the Commission's
work.

13/ The task forces, in alphabetical order, were: Budget
and Accounting; Committee on Business Organizations of the Department of Defense; Depot Utilization; Federal Activities Competitive
with Private Enterprise; Intelligence Activities; Legal Services
and Procedure; Lending, Guaranteeing, and Insurance Activities;
Medical Services; Military Procurement; Overseas Economic Operations; Paperwork Management; Personnel and Civil Service; Personnel
Problems in the Department of Defense; Real Property Management;
Research and Development; Subsistence Services (Food and Clothing);
Transportation; Use and Disposal of Federal Surplus Property; and
Water Resources and Power.

14/ MacNeil and Metz, The Hoover Report: 1953-1955, p. 17.

15/ Fesler, "Administrative Literature and the Second Hoover Commission Reports," p. 143.

16/ MacNeil and Metz, The Hoover Report: 1953-1955, p. 17.

17/ Herbert Emmerich remarked critically upon the relatively few persons selected from the academic community for task forces or their staffs. The task forces, in his view, were not balanced.

A much greater imbalance characterized the composition of the task forces and special committees of the second commission. Perhaps the Brownlow Committee erred on the side of appointing too many political scientists on its staff, and Hoover I had a good many of them in key positions, but Hoover II was practically uncontaminated in this respect. Out of 150 persons I can identify only 6 in this category. Its task forces were heavily weighted with representatives of business and the professions who could hardly have been called 'disinterested' on problems so largely concerned with busienss and government.

(Federal Organization and Administrative Management, p. 109)

18/ William R. Divine, "The Second Hoover Commission Report: An Analysis," Public Administration Review 15 (Autumn 1955), p. 267.

19/ MacNeil and Metz, The Hoover Report: 1953-1955, p. 22.

20/ Ibid., pp. 19, 20.

21/ Fesler, "Administrative Literature and the Second Hoover Commission Reports," p. 151.

22/ Only one task force report, Business Organization of the Department of Defense, was accepted without revision ("so succinct that it cannot be condensed") by the Commission and forwarded to Congress as its own report.

23/ MacNeil and Metz, The Hoover Report: 1953-1955, p. 21.

24/ Ibid.

25/ Unlike the first Commission, which decided not to make an "official" estimate of savings possible from implementation of its recommendations, the second Commission did go on record with a "savings estimate." "The primary purpose of the Commission was to recommend methods by which savings could be made in the expenditures of the agencies of the executive branch . . . ." Although the figures provided by most task forces were admittedly "soft," they were both substantial and controversial. The estimate was over $8 billion. Second Commission, Final Report, pp. 19-20.

26/ Second Commission, Final Report, pp. 26-31. Commissioner Chet Holifield stated:

> This Commission, and others like it, obtain the funds because they enjoy great prestige and command national attention. The justification for existence, however, is that they are supposed to bring to bear the dispassionate and considered judgment of a select group of men on matters of great national concern which transcend party differences.
> The value of the Commission is nullified if its scope of inquiry is not carefully defined and if the attribute of bi-partisanship is absent.
> The Hoover Commission, in its second round of endeavor, is wanting on both counts. (p. 27)

27/ Ibid., p. 15.

28/ Congress, House, Summary of . . . First and Second Hoover Commissions (1963), p. 13.

29/ There were two post-hoc attempts to categorize the Commission's reports. MacNeil and Metz "found the reports made a pattern" and they organized their book under four subject headings: The Tools of Government; Big Government; The Big Spender; and Overseas Economic Development. MacNeil and Metz, The Hoover Report: 1953-1955, p. 24. Fesler offered a somewhat more scholarly typology: Government as Government; Government as Business; and Government as Policy. Fesler, "Administrative Literature and the Second Hoover Commission," pp. 149-150.

30/ Citizens Committee for the Hoover Report, Final Report, October 1958, p. 5.
The Senate Committee on Government Operations in its 1958 summary implementation report found the figure of 314 recommendations too general in coverage and determined that there were actually 519 separate recommendations. "This includes the numbered recommendations, lettered subdivisions of recommendations, such as recommendation 1(a) and 1(b), etc.; task force recommendations which the Commission specifically endorsed, and certain textual recommendations which the Commission did not number." U.S., Congress, Senate, Committee on Government Operations, Action by the Congress and the Executive Branch of the Government on the Second Hoover Commission Reports, 1955-1957, S.Rept. 1289, 85th Cong., 2d sess., 1958, p. 1.

31/ Divine, "The Second Hoover Commission Report: An Analysis," p. 266. Of the 314 recommendations that the second Hoover Commission eventually forwarded to Congress, when Mr. Hoover was asked which one he thought the most important, he was reported to have replied without hesitation: "I would pick the recommendation for the setting up a senior civil service." MacNeil and Metz, The Hoover Report: 1953-1955, p. 29.

32/ The Commission used the term "noncareer executive" to cover
all appointees of the President confirmed by the Senate; appointees
of the President not confirmed by the Senate; and other officials
who are appointed and serve at the pleasure of department and agency
heads to positions excepted from the civil service laws. The term
did not include junior aides, private secretaries and other persons
in close personal and confidential relationships to department heads
and other top agency officials.

33/ Second Commission, Personnel and Civil Service, p. 44.

34/ Leonard White, a foremost public administration scholar and
member of the Personnel Task Force offered the following analysis of
what the Commission was seeking in its proposal for a Senior Civil
Service:

> A general is a general, in full possession of rank,
> emoluments, and status whether he is in command of a
> division or army in the field, stationed at a garrison
> at home or on occupation duty, sitting behind a desk
> in Washington with duties large or small, or awaiting
> orders. He may be assigned to various types of mission,
> to varying responsibilities, at any place. His status,
> nevertheless, is unchanged and he is subject to removal
> only by court-martial. Applying these standards to
> high-ranking civil officers, it would follow that an
> incoming administration would have available a corps
> of highly qualified civilian executives with protected
> status, ready for assignment wherever the political
> command thought advisable. These officials would,
> however, have no claim to their existing positions;
> if the incoming agency head found any one of them
> incompatible, he would be free to cause a transfer
> elsewhere, but not removal from the service. Some
> central way station, such as the Bureau of the Budget
> or the General Services Administration, would be neces-
> sary to facilitate the task of reassignment.

(Leonard D. White, Introduction to the Study of Public
Administration, 4th ed. (New York: Macmillan Company,
1955), p. 330.)

35/ Second Commission, Personnel and Civil Service, p. 41.

36/ Among the articles generated by the controversy over the
establishment of a Senior Civil Service are: Leonard D. White, "The
Senior Civil Service," Public Administration Review 15 (Autumn 1955):
237-243. Leonard D. White, "The Case for the Senior Civil Service,"
Personnel Administration 19 (January/ February 1966): 4-9. Herman M.
Somers, "Some Reservations About the Senior Civil Service," Personnel
Administration 19 (January/ February, 1956): 10-18. Everett Reimer,
"The Case Against the Senior Civil Service," Personnel Administration

(continued) 19 (March/April 1956): 31-40. Paul Van Riper, "The Senior Civil Service and the Career System," Public Administration Review 18 (Summer 1958): 189-200.

37/ For an informative discussion of the competing views on the role of the executive in the Federal Government in light of the second Hoover Commission's personnel and management recommendations, see: Marver Bernstein, The Job of the Federal Executive (Washington: The Brookings Institution, 1959).

38/ Herbert Kaufman, "The Growth of the Federal Personnel System," IN The Federal Government Service, Wallace Sayre, ed. (Englewood Cliffs, New Jersey: Prentice-Hall, 1965), p. 66.

39/ U.S., Congress, House, Committee on Post Office and Civil Service, Legislative History of the Civil Service Reform Act of 1978, 2v, Committee print, 96th Cong., 1st sess., 1979.
      The Senior Executive Service, while still young, has al-ready undergone considerable travail, see: Bruce Buchanan, "The Senior Executive Service: How Can We Tell If It Works?" Public Administration Review 41 (May/June 1981): 349-358.

40/ An insightful public law history of the evolution of the executive budgetary process is provided in Louis Fisher, Presidential Spending Power (Princeton: Princeton University Press, 1975).

41/ Second Commission, Task Force Report on Budget and Account-ing, p. 31.

42/ Fisher, Presidential Spending Power, p. 78ff.

43/ Second Commission, Budget and Accounting, p. 7.

44/ Ibid., p. 25.

45/ One of the dissenting Commissioners, James Farley, argued:

      This report has been approached from the viewpoint of a
      cost accountant operating in a private commercial enterprise,
      in which goods and services are produced and sold for the
      avowed purpose of providing a profit for those whose capital is
      invested. This may be an appropriate concept for governmental
      operations which are similar to private commercial ventures
      and, in fact, is currently in use by many such governmental
      organizations as stated in the report, it does not seem to me,
      however, to be appropriate across-the-board to all Government
      activities and operations. (Ibid., pp. 69-70)

46/ Fisher, Presidential Spending Power, pp. 135-137.

47/ Ibid., p. 138.

48/ Second Commission, Final Report, pp. 19-20.

49/ The chairman of the task force on Budget and Accounting, J. Harold Stewart, acknowledged that his task force had issued this estimate but argued that it was not intended to be ascribed to simply changing the accounting system. What the task force had done was to estimate, arbitrarily, that the Commission recommendations, if adopted in toto, would save ten percent of the "controllable budget," or $4.8 billion of the $48 billion in controllable items. Since this figure appeared too precise, "the general agreement was that we should say $4 billion." J. Harold Stewart, "The Hoover Commission Recommendations on Budgeting and Accounting," The Federal Accountant 7 (March 1958): 8-10.

50/ Statement of Herbert Hoover to the Task Force on Legal Services and Procedures, February 5, 1954. "The whole field is open to you—and you are free to undertake investigations and make recommendations on any subject in the legal field, as far as the executive branch of Government is concerned." Second Commission, Task Force Report on Legal Services and Procedures, p. 1.

51/ William Divine, "The Second Hoover Commission Reports: An Analysis," Public Administration Review 15 (Autumn 1955), p. 267.

52/ Second Commission, Legal Services and Procedures, p. 5.

53/ The Commission stated: "A plain, simple, and prompt judicial remedy should be made available for every legal wrong resulting from agency action or inaction, except where Congress expressly precludes judicial review." Ibid., p. 75.

54/ Herbert Emmerich observed that the recommendations of the Commission with respect to legal services and procedures favored greater insulation of regulatory agencies from political accountability. "In calling for still further independence of these highly autonomous commissions, they were a move for complete divorcement from presidential influence and control, the need for which the Brownlow Committee had emphasized and Hoover I had acknowledged." Federal Organization and Administration Management, p. 117.

55/ Commissioner Holifield perceived that the recommendations of the Legal Services and Procedures report constituted an attempt to insulate the legal profession in the Federal service from political accountability to Congress.

The drift of the Commission recommendations is to 'judicialize' procedures in the administrative agencies as much as possible and to go even further in breaking off some judicial-type functions and placing them in an administrative court. To the extent that the proposed changes in administrative procedure seek a basic shift of administrative power to the courts or offer loopholes for thwarting agency action in carrying out congressional policies, I must record my objections."

(continued) (Second Commission, Legal Services and Procedures, p. 111)

56/ Second Commission, Business Organization of the Department of Defense, p. 45.

57/ Reports on Surplus Property; Real Property Management; Transportation; Depot Utilization; and Food Clothing.

58/ The report on Paperwork Management was replete with statistical "horror stories." The task force spoke in somewhat dated graphic terms on the immensity of the paperwork problem. "In the past 40 years, the number of letters produced by the Federal Government each year has increased sixty-fold to well over 1 billion. It is difficult for most people to comprehend the quantities of mail coming out of Government offices. A billion letters ready for mailing and stacked one on the other would reach 390 miles into the stratosphere, some 25 times higher than man has flown." Second Commission, Task Force on Paperwork Management, Part I, p. 13.
For a brief history of "paperwork management" over the years culminating in the Paperwork Reduction Act of 1980 (94 Stat. 2812), see U.S., Commission of Federal Paperwork, History of Paperwork Reform Efforts (Washington: U.S., Govt. Print. Off., 1977). Also; U.S., Congress, Senate Committee on Governmental Affairs, Paperwork Reduction Act of 1980, S. Rept. 930, 96th Cong., 2d sess., 1980. There is no mention of the second Commission's paperwork management report in either report.

59/ Emmerich, Federal Organization and Administrative Management, p. 119.

60/ Second Commission, Business Enterprises, p. xi.

61/ Ibid., pp. xii-xiii.

62/ Ibid., p. 82.

63/ Second Commission, Lending, Guaranteeing, and Insurance Activities.

64/ Ibid., p. 9.

65/ Ibid., p. 12.

66/ Ellis W. Hawley, "Herbert Hoover, the Commerce Secretariat, and the Vision of an Associative State, 1921-1928," Journal of American History 61 (June 1974): 116-140.

67/ Commissioner Chet Holifield, in his usual dissenting mode, noted that whatever the advantages of mutualization, these hybrid entities are (in most instances) privately owned and managed, and therefore subject to only a limited amount of Government regulation, (continued) tenuous accountability to the President and Congress, and are often exempt from General Accounting Office audit control.

> At the same time the 'mutualized' agencies enjoy many Government privileges. Among these are tax exemptions, free use of Government mails, free use of Government buildings and property, Government annuity contributions to the employees, access to Government funds and reliance upon Government insurance or other commitments.
> Even if these privileges are removed in whole or in part, the agencies are still Federal instrumentalities in some sense, and the conflict of interest between private and public management and policy remains. (Ibid., pp. 121-122).

68/ For a discussion of wholly-owned Government corporations and mixed-ownership Government enterprises, See National Academy of Public Administration, Report on Government Corporation, 2v. (Washington: National Academy of Public Administration, 1981).

69/ The first Hoover Commission had recommended the liquidation of the Reconstruction Finance Corporation (RFC). Various scandals involving RFC lending practices were highlighted in the press and in a Senate investigation in 1951 which set the stage for Congress to pass the Reconstruction Finance Corporation Liquidation Act in 1953. Although the RFC was finally liquidated in 1957, some of its programs were transferred to other agencies, notably the new Small Business Administration.

70/ "Such competition by the Government with private enterprise in the power field is more extensive than in any other governmental field and has taken on many aspects which are a negation of our fundamental economic system." Second Commission, Water Resources and Power, v. 1, p. 115.

71/ Aaron Wildavsky, "TVA and Power Politics," American Political Science Review 55 (September 1961): 576-590.

72/ Second Commission, Water Resources and Power, v. 1, pp. 36-37.

73/ It was not universally agreed that these prescriptive statements constituted a national water use policy. Commissioner Chet Holifield, for one, did not believe that they did. "Even though the Commission jumps squarely into the policy field," Holifield argued, "its 'nine points' listed in Recommendation 1 do not add up to a 'national water policy' for which the Commission asserts there is an imperative need. Some of the points are pious but ambiguous expressions; others are generally accepted in present practice." Second Commission, Water Resources and Power, v. 2, p. 11.
It should also be noted that the Commission's Report on Water Resources and Power was split into two volumes. The second volume consisted solely of separate statements by Commissioners.

(continued) Commissioner Chet Holifield's dissent constituted 84 of the 94 pages of this volume.

74/ For an extended analysis of the water resources recommendations of both Hoover Commissions, and other advisory groups functioning during the same period, see James Fesler, "National Water Resources Administration," IN Economics and Public Policy in Water Resources Development (Ames, Iowa: Iowa State University Press, 1964): 368-402. Fesler's essay explores the problems advisory commissions encounter when they try to suggest how agencies should be reorganized without having themselves a coherent or consistent "organizing concept."

75/ U.S., President's Commission on Water Resources Policy, Report (Washington: U.S. Govt. Print. Off., 1950), p. 49.
The creation of a broadly-based Department of Natural Resources has long been a popular proposal emanating from individuals and advisory commissions. See, Fesler, "National Water Resources Administration," p. 395.

76/ Albert Stone offered the following critical assessment of the recommendations:

These recommendations result in very few changes: (1) the only shifts in agency responsibility among the twenty-five agencies are the shift of one function from the Soil Conservation Service to the Corps of Engineers, and the grouping of hydrologic data functions; (2) there are two fiscal changes, both of minor importance; (3) federal power systems will have increased independence, but will still be numbered among the twenty-five overlapping and conflicting agencies; (4) the amount of governmental review of proposed projects will be increased; and (5) a twenty-sixth agency, the Water Resources Board will be created, presumably to work out all of the difficult problems.
The net result is that the Commission has very little to say about one of its major tasks, and has recommended the creation of another agency to which it has bequeathed that task. Apparently, this Hoover Commission disapproves of the conclusions reached by the 1947 Hoover Commission.

(Albert Stone, "The Hoover Reports on Water Resources and Power: A Commentary," California Law Review 43 (December 1955), pp. 752-73.

77/ Emmerich, Federal Organization and Administrative Management, p. 114.

78/ The Commission was apparently of the belief that there was little distinctive about the role of the Department of State in foreign economic affairs. The functions performed by the State Department and its employees could be handled equally well by many units of the Government.

"A considerable number of the Foreign Operations Administration staff might be transferred to the agencies mentioned above. The problem of providing for the qualified remainder is not one of great proportions. The whole staff now is about 4,200 Americans and the annual turnover of the Federal civil employees exceeds 500,000 per annum."

(Second Commission, Overseas Economic Operations, p. 61.)

79/ Second Commission, Federal Medical Services, p. 25.

80/ Herbert Emmmerich provided the following assessment of two of the recommendations to create new advisory units in the Executive Office.

Two questions might be raised about these two top-level recommendations [water resources and health policy] in the field of governmental reorganization. The minor question is whether the commission was not really throwing it hands up in the case of these two comlex fields and, instead of recommending new policies and a rearrangement of agency functions and structures, was simply passing the buck to two coordinating councils. But the more important question was whether these bodies, consisting of a large number of part-time outsiders, was intended to assist the President in the coordination of many scattered and conflicting programs, or whether they were really meant to surround the President in fields in which the commission believed there was an excess of governmental activity. Given the orientation of the commission and its task forces, it is hard to avoid the conclusion that the two recommendations were essentially devices to place the public business of water resources and health policy in private hands.

(Federal Organization and Administrative Management, p. 114)

81/ Second Commission, Research and Development in the Government, p. 47.

82/ Ibid., p. 50.

83/ MacNeil and Metz, The Hoover Report: 1953-1955, p. 310.

84/ Citizens Committee for the Hoover Report, "Final Report," Reorganization News, October 1958, p. 5.

85/ MacNeil and Metz, The Hoover Report: 1953-1955, p. 299.

86/ Fesler, "Administrative Literature and the Second Hoover Commission Report," p. 144.

87/ Emmerich, Federal Organization and Administrative Management, p. 124.

88/ Presidents Hoover and Eisenhower have both undergone extensive scholarly reassessment of their presidential tenures and their personal leadership qualities. In the case of Dwight Eisenhower, the reassessment, begun in the late 1970s, has resulted in a positive revision of the opinion widely shared in the academic community regarding his abilities as a political leader. Rather than the "aging hero" image portrayed in the books written during the 1950s and 1960s, e.g., Richard Neustadt's Presidential Power, John Wiley and Sons, 1960, the newer, "revisionist" writings stress Eisenhower's performance as an astute political practitioner.
A close study of the original documents of his Administration suggest a President whose activism was subtle, but effective. Eisenhower preferred informal to formal means of influence. With respect to the second Hoover Commission, he chose to "end-run" it rather than confront and oppose the Commission and its recommendations. The results, however, were nearly the same. For a revisionist perspective on Eisenhower, see Fred Greenstein, "Eisenhower as an Activist President: A Look at New Evidence, Political Science Quarterly 94 (Winter 1979-80): 575-600. Also, Herbert S. Parmet, Eisenhower and the American Crusades (New York: Macmillan Company, 1972).

89/ "Democrats who campaigned successfully against 'Hooverism' for 20 long years are gaily looking forward to a repeat performance in 1956." "Hoover Policies: Commission has Stirred Congressional Wrath By Seeking Changes in Federal Programs," Congressional Quarterly, June 17, 1955. p. 692.

90/ Divine, The Second Hoover Commission Report, p. 269.

91/ Fesler, "Administrative Literature and the Second Hoover Commission Reports," p. 157.

92/ Harold Seidman discusses Government agencies as social institutions with distinctive cultures and personalities. He emphasizes the role of professions in determining the cultural norms of agencies. Politics, Position, and Power, 3d ed., chapter 6. Also; Frederick C. Mosher, Democracy and the Public Service (New York: Oxford University Press, 1968), chapter 4.

93/ Peri Arnold, "Leviathan Domesticated: An Exploration Into the Relationship Between Administrative Theory and the Positive State." Paper delivered at the National Conference of the American Society for Public Administration, April 13-16, San Francisco, California, p. 28.

94/   After a brief and controversial stint as Director of the Voice of America in 1953, Robert Johnson had returned as President of Temple University from whence he retired in 1959.

95/   "Back To McKinley," Washington Post, July 4, 1955, p. 14.

96/   Richard L. Strout, "Hoover Task Force Proposed Breakup of TVA: 'Leaked' Report Triggers Congress Explosion," Christian Science Monitor, May 18, 1955, p. 3.

97/   "Neuberger Defies G.O.P. To Present Hoover Bills, New York Times, August 19, 1955, p. A-11.

98/   Citizens Committee for the Hoover Report, Reorganization News, October 1957, p. 4.

99/   Citizens Committee for the Hoover Report, Background Information, n.d., p. 3.

100/   Citizens Committee for the Hoover Report, "Final Report," Reorganization News, October, 1958.

4
The Commissions in Retrospect

If the issuance of the 1937 Brownlow Committee report can be described as the "high noon of orthodoxy in public administration theory in the United States," 1/ then the issuance of the Hoover Commission reports can be reasonably identified as the "Indian summer" of orthodoxy. The allusion to Indian summer appears appropriate because with the Hoover Commission reports orthodoxy enjoyed a brief respite from the heavy attacks to which it had been subjected in the immediate post-War years. 2/

When the attack on orthodoxy resumed, the assault was no longer frontal but rather consisted of flanking movements. Other theories of varying inclusivity appeared, acquired adherents, then with expectations unfulfilled they became assimilated into the intellectual history of public administration. 3/ Indeed, most of what passed as theory in public administration was middle-range in scope and as culture bound as the old orthodox theory. While it is tempting and easy to disparage the orthodox doctrines, it was not so easy to come up with a better theory. This point is well-stated by Harold Seidman, himself a critic of orthodoxy, with respect to Federal organization and management.

> While the observations on the discrepencies between the dogmas and the facts of organizational life and behavior are pertinent and valid, these do not add up to a rational well-articulated set of working hypotheses for dealing with the present and emerging problems of federal organization. It is easy to pick the flaws in the concepts of unity of command, straight lines of authority and accountability, and organization by major purpose; it is far more difficult to develop acceptable alternatives . . . .
> Flawed and imperfect as they may be, the orthodox 'principles' remain the only simple, readily understood, and comprehensive set of guidelines available to the President and the Congress for resolving the problems of executive branch structure. 4/

The two Commissions shared many characteristics. Both were established by statute with the impetus for creation coming from Congress, not the President. Many congressional sponsors envisioned these Commissions as central to a counterstrategy against the expanding institutional presidency. The Commissions were "citizens commissions" although their membership included persons selected from among officeholders. The selection process was "mixed" in that appointments were made by both the leadership of Congress and the President. They were bipartisan, although the requirement for bipartisanship was missing from the enabling statute of the second Commission. They were both episodic, or temporary, bodies, meaning that they had a definite life span, a little over two years, submitted their reports, and disbanded.

Both Commissions had the same Chairman, Herbert Hoover. Hoover was an aggressive Chairman who devoted more time and energy to the Commission than any of the other members. The central staff, although small in both instances, was really his staff and not readily available to the other Commissioners.

Hoover's ideas on government structure and management comprised an unusual blend. He wanted Federal promotion of industry, yet was opposed to the Federal Government becoming directly responsible for the performance of many functions. He believed that business and government should become partners in ventures, "mutualization" the second Commission would call it, yet he feared Federal dominance. He wanted less Federal Government intervention in the social and economic life of the Nation, yet believed in a "strong" presidency. Hoover had faith that many of the problems besetting government could be solved if the views of "experts" could be brought to bear rather than those of the politicans.

The Commissions were fairly homogeneous bodies. They consisted of 12 men of senior years who had experience in the Federal Government. They were not selected as "representatives" of particular interest groups or constituencies. The Commissions were not "representative bodies," rather they were "blue-ribbon panels" selected for "expertise" and experience, not for their potential constituency support. There was a high degree of consensus among the members even before the Commissions met. Most of the Commissioners were adept at compromise. Few disputes followed partisan lines.

As with most commissions and committees, some members worked hard, others worked rarely. Some were sophisticated in their understanding of government organization, others relatively unsophisticated, or easily led. 5/ The important point to recognize about the membership is that once the selection was made, the choice of issues and agencies to study, and the recommendations to be forthcoming, was largely preordained. There were few surprises.

The paucity of members and staff from the academic community
was evident both in the quantity and quality of the reports,
particularly with respect to the second Commission. 6/ The reports, heavily influenced by the writing style of Mr. Hoover himself,
were written like press releases, short and terse. Compound sentences were noteworthy by their infrequent use. The quality of the
reports, on the other hand, varied and sometimes bordered on the
simplistic. Both Commissions offered major and trivial recommendations side-by-side, with little distinction. Recognition of prior
studies or scholarly works on the subjects under consideration was
rare.

There were several contrasts between the first and second Commissions, as well as similarities. The first Commission wrote its
reports in the aftermath of the War. There were a number of relatively obvious and noncontroversial problems that needed to be addressed. Agencies and programs geared to the Depression and fighting
the War could be phased-out or reorganized. Certain managerial laws,
e.g., procurement laws, could be changed to strengthen the presidential review process without engendering stiff resistance. These were
the easy "reforms."

Between the first and second Commission, however, came the
Korean War. The Korean War altered the budget and tilted it toward
the military. Administrative policies and programs became more
complex with greater reliance placed upon categorical grants-in-aid.
As noted in the discussion of the second Commission, the mid-1950s,
notwithstanding the basically conservative philosophy of the Eisenhower Administration, were years when Federal Government intervention
in the public and private sectors had wide support. The second Commission differed significantly from the first Commission simply because it seemed to be "out-of-tune" with the dominant mood of the
time. Also, the first Hoover Commission was a difficult act to follow and high expectations by the media led to understandable disappointment with the comparatively modest recommendations offered by
the second Commission.

The two Commissions viewed their mandates differently. The
first Commission, initially at least, considered its mandate
broadly and was prepared to recommend the "elimination" of certain
functions of government, clearly entering thereby the policy or
legislative arena. Possibly it was not coincidental that the Commission, through its Chairman, announced shortly after the 1948
presidential election results were tallied, that it had determined
to narrow its mandate to management issues. "Our job," Chairman
Hoover replied to a press inquiry, "is to make every government
activity that now exists work efficiently. I take it that major
functions of the Government are determinable as needed by the Congress. It is not our function to say whether it should exist or not,
but it is our function to see if we cannot make it work better."

The second Commission, on the other hand, did not limit its field of interest to management issues. It was prepared to offer policy recommendations that would lead to less government intervention in the public and private sectors. The result, in the opinion of most observers, was a less useful set of reports.

A final major difference between the Commissions lay in the underlying assumptions guiding their work. The first Commission had an administrative model in mind of what the executive branch ought to look like. The second Commission had no such model. This was a critical distinction, as James Fesler concluded:

> The [second] Commission provides no administrative
> model; the Brownlow Committee and the first Hoover Com-
> mission did provide such a model and one could decide
> whether he liked it or not. The vacuum is not adequately
> filled by the Commission's efforts to state its objectives.
> The principal explicit statement provides a mixture of
> goals (national security, fundamental research, private
> enterprise, common welfare, and strengthening of
> 'the economic, social and governmental structure which
> has brought us, now for 166 years, constant blessings
> and progress') and means (efficiency, elimination of
> waste, elimination or reduction of government competition
> with private enterprise), but the means are actually
> treated as ends valuable in themselves so long as they
> do not war with other ends . . . ." 7/

The first Commission visualized the ideal executive branch as one in which most agencies and functions were placed within departments with secretaries of the departments reporting to the President as chief manager. Primary program authorities would be centralized in the secretaries and delegated to them. No such model is evident in the second Commission reports. The second Commission was displeased to find the heads of 64 agencies reporting directly to the President. "Of these, the President has the unavoidable direct responsibility for about 31, but the remaining 33 are of such diverse character and duties that the few of them lend themselves to relocation in other existing agencies." 8/ Therefore, the Commission recommended that these agencies be required to "report regularly upon such matters as organizational activities, proposed programs, appointments of staff, expenditures and their proposed appropriations" to a designated official, presumably in the Executive Office of the President. The implications of such a recommendation, if it had been accepted, are obviously profound, yet went undiscussed by the Commission. This constituted the only general commentary on the organizational arrangements of the executive branch by the second Commission.

Neither Commission played a role in the growth of the conservative intellectual movement in the post-War period. 9/ The several concepts that influenced the Commissions' recommendations, e.g., "economy and efficiency," were clearly instrumental values left over from the Progressive Era. The Commissions were conservative only in the sense that a majority of the members were disposed towards a less interventionist Government and a smaller Federal budget. In some quarters, the Commissions have been viewed as intellectually naive because while they voiced their opposition to "big government," their recommendations were designed to result in substantial increments of power to political executives, most notably the President.

The reports of the task forces and the Commission give little hint of the conceptual breakthroughs that were about to occur in social science and administrative methodology and research. There was little in the way of program analysis or of suggestions as to ways and means of testing program effectiveness. In intellectual terms, therefore, the Commission reports were largely anachronistic when they appeared and provided few clues about the trends that would result in a massive Federal apparatus by the late 1970s.

While legitimate criticisms may be lodged against the Commissions and their reports for the absence of prescience regarding future intellectual trends, it is also appropriate to recognize some of the Commissions' strengths. The two Hoover Commissions were important milestones in American administrative history and contributed substantially to the evolution of the Federal executive establishment. The lasting contribution of the two Commissions, and here the credit must rest largely with the first Commission, is to be found in the intellectual support given to the concept of the institutional presidency as manager of Government and to the notion of departmentalism.

Regarding the institutional presidency, the first Commission was very much an heir to the Brownlow Committee of twelve years before. The Commission, and particularly the Chairman, envisioned the President as manager of a massive enterprise and, as adherents of orthodox administrative theory, they believed a manager should be given authority commensurate with his responsibilities.

In retrospect, the executive branch appears to have been reasonably well-managed during the 1940s and 1950s. The managerial agencies, e.g., Bureau of the Budget, were at the zenith of their strength. While a number of factors might be cited as contributing to this felicitous situation, it would be unfair and inaccurate to ignore the contribution of the two Hoover Commissions. The first Commission, in particular, argued from first principles stressing the need for political and managerial accountability and clear lines of responsibility and control. All proposals for change, in their view, should be measured by whether or not they enhance those values.

The influence of the Hoover Commissions and their administrative philosophy lasted just about a decade. Beginning in the mid-1960s, and accelerating during the 1970s, the concept of departmentalism underwent erosion. 10/ Agencies and government enterprises located outside the executive departments began to be created with frequency and awarded considerable autonomy. 11/ Many additional managerial laws and regulations were passed, e.g., Freedom of Information Act, regulatory review processes, each limiting managerial discretion and authority. Even the institutionalized presidency has undergone substantial reductions in its authorities and resources.

Given the fact that the Hoover Commissions met during a different, and simpler, period, what can be learned from their experience that may assist us today? Harold Seidman is addressing this question when he states: "The principles of organization advanced by the Hoover Commission have not lost their validity, but read by themselves they do not contribute materially to our understanding of current problems of government organization and management." 12/

The Hoover Commissions were one generation's attempt to respond to certain perennial questions, most notably: "Who should be held responsible by the electorate for managing the executive functions of the Federal Government?" The Hoover Commissions answered this question by stating that the electorate should hold the President responsible and in return should be prepared to give him the authority and resources to meet this responsibility. In subsequent years, however, we have retreated from this position with Congress, the courts, independent commissions, and private contractors all being assigned increased roles in administrative management. 13/ This shift in the focus of managerial power and responsibility away from the institutional presidency has had consequences on how the executive branch is organized and how well is functions.

The Hoover Commissions met at a time when there was considerable consensus about how the Government ought to be organized and run and what it ought to be doing. For a "citizens commission" to be successful, there must be in advance a working consensus among the members regarding what theory, or model, of Government they are seeking. And there must be some agreement regarding the questions they as a Commission should ask. Whether such a consensus exists today, or is emerging as a result of the 1980 presidential election, is a critical question that must be addressed prior to useful speculation as to the possible success of a similar Commission in this decade.

1/ Wallace Sayre, "Premises of Public Administration: Past and Emerging," Public Administration Review 18 (Spring 1958), p. 103.

2/ See, for example, Herbert Simon, Administrative Behavior (New York: Macmillam Company, 1947).

3/ For a discussion of recent intellectual trends in public administration, particularly in the post-orthodoxy period, see, Alan Altshuler, "The Study of American Public Administration," in The Politics of the Federal Bureaucracy, Alan Altshuler, editor (New (continued) York: Dodd, Mead and Company, 1968), pp. 55-72. Also, Dwight Waldo, The Enterprise of Public Administration: A Summary View (Novato, California: Chandler Sharp Publishers, Inc., 1980).

4/ Harold Seidman, Politics, Position and Power, 3d ed. (New York: Oxford University Press, 1980), pp. 8-9.

5/ The internal sociology of commissions has occasioned some research. Although not specifically concerned with the two Hoover Commissions, insights into the internal workings of presidential com- missions in general may be found: Mirra Komarovsky, editor, Sociology and Public Policy: The Case of Presidential Commissions (New York; Elsevier, 1975).

6/ "Perhaps the Brownlow Committee erred on the side of ap- pointing too many political scientists on its staff, and Hoover I had a good many of them in key positions, but Hoover II was practically uncontaminated in this respect. Out of 150 persons I can identify only 6 in this category." Emmerich, Federal Organization and Admin- istrative Management, p. 109.

7/ Fesler, "Administrative Literature and the Second Hoover Commission Reports," p. 150.

8/ Second Hoover Commission, Final Report, p. 17.

9/ A detailed description and analysis of the many faceted con- servative intellectual movement between the years 1945 and 1975 does not mention either of the two Hoover Commissions. George H. Nash, The Conservative Intellectual Movement in America, Since 1945 (New York: Basic Books, Inc., 1976).

10/ For a discussion of organizational trends in the Federal Government since the two Hoover Commissions, see: U.S., Senate, Committee on Governmental Affairs, The Federal Executive Establish- ment: Evolution and Trends, Committee print, prepared by Ronald C. Moe, Congressional Research Service, 96th Cong., 2d sess., 1980.

11/ Lloyd D. Musolf and Harold Seidman. "The Blurred Lines of Public Administration," Public Administration Review 40 (March/ April 1980): 124-130. National Academy of Public Administration, Report on Government Corporations, 2v. (Washington: National Academy of Public Administration, 1981).

12/ Seidman, Politics, Position, and Power, 3d ed., p. 328.

13/ Louis Fisher, in several writings, contends that it is pointless to try making the President the sole manager of the execu- tive branch. "It seems idle at this point to pretend that we can place all governmental functions neatly in three separate branches, keeping legislation in Congress, administration in the executive (continued) branch, and adjudication in the courts. We cannot even distinguish, with any clarity, between federal and state or between public and private. For two centuries we have veered off down a separate road, allocating administrative functions to an ever growing number of autonomous commissions, administrative bodies, the courts, congressional committees, and advisory groups. If it were possible, at one fell swoop, to return all administrative powers overnight to the President, the process of decentralization would begin at dawn the following day." "The Administrative State: A Panoramic View," paper presented at the Planning Meeting for the Garfield Foundation, November 13-14, 1981, Princeton, New Jersey, p. 43. See, also: Fisher, "Congress and the President in the Administrative Process: The Uneasy Alliance," in Hugh Heclo and Lester M. Salamon, eds., The Illusion of Presidential Government (Boulder: Colorado, Westview Press, 1981), pp. 21-43.

Bibliography

BOOKS

Appleby, Paul. <u>Policy and Administration</u>. University, Alabama: University of Alabama Press, 1949.

Bernstein, Marver H. <u>Regulating Business By Independent Commission</u>. Westpoint, Conn: Greenwood Press, 1977, c. 1955.

_____ <u>The Job of the Federal Executive</u>. Washington: Brookings Institution, 1958.

Brownlow, Louis. <u>A Passion For Anonymity</u>. 2v. Chicago: University of Chicago Press, 1958.

Burner, David. <u>Herbert Hoover: A Public Life</u>. New York: Alfred A. Knopf, 1979.

Caraley, Demetrios. <u>The Politics of Military Unification</u>. New York: Columbia University Press, 1966.

Cronin, Thomas F., and Greenberg, Sanford B., comps. <u>The Presidential Advisory System</u>. New York: Harper and Row, 1969.

Cushman, Robert E. <u>The Independent Regulatory Commissions</u>. New York: Oxford University Press, 1941.

Emmerich, Herbert. <u>Federal Organization and Administrative Management</u>. University, Alabama: University of Alabama Press, 1971.

_____ <u>Essays on Federal Reorganization</u>. University, Alabama: University of Alabama Press, 1950.

Fenno, Richard. <u>The President's Cabinet: An Analysis In the Period From Wilson to Eisenhower</u>. Cambridge: Harvard University Press, 1959. (Harvard political studies)

131

Fisher, Louis. Presidential Spending Power. Princeton: Princeton
    University Press, 1975. 345 p.

Gervasi, Frank. Big Government: The Meaning and Purpose of the
    Hoover Commission Report. New York: McGraw-Hill Book Company,
    1949.

Goldberg, Sidney, and Seidman, Harold. The Government Corporation:
    Elements of a Model Charter. Chicago: Public Administration
    Press, 1953.

Gulick, Luther, and Urwick, L., eds. Papers on the Science of Ad-
    ministration. New York: A.M. Kelly, 1969, c1937.

Harris, Joseph P. Congressional Control of Administration. Wash-
    ington: Brookings Institution, 1964.

Hobbs, Edward H. Executive Reorganization in the National Govern-
    ment. Oxford, Mississippi: University of Mississippi Press,
    1953.

Hoover, Herbert. The Memoirs of Herbert Hoover: Years of Adventure,
    1874-1920. New York: Macmillan Co., 1951.

Karl, Barry Dean. Executive Reorganization and Reform in the New
    Deal, the Genesis of Administrative Management, 1900-1939. Cam-
    bridge: Harvard University Press, 1963.

Kaufman, Herbert. Are Governmental Organizations Immortal? Wash-
    ington: Brookings Institution, 1976.

_____ The Limits of Organizational Change. University: Uni-
    versity of Alabama Press, 1971.

Komarovsky, Mirra, ed. Sociology and Public Policy: The Case of
    Presidential Commissions. New York: Elsevier, 1975.

Lloyd, Craig. Aggressive Introvert: A Study of Herbert Hoover and
    Public Relations Management, 1912-1932. Columbus: Ohio State
    University Press, 1972.

MacNeil, Neil and Metz, Harold. The Hoover Report, 1953-1955: What
    it Means to You as Citizen and Taxpayer. New York: Macmillan
    Company, 1956.

Maass, Arthur. Muddy Waters; the Army Engineers and the Nation's
    Rivers. Cambridge, Harvard University Press, 1951.

Meriam, Lewis and Schmeckebier, Lawrence F. Reorganization of the
    National Government; What Does It Involve? Washington: Brook-
    ings Institution, 1939.

Myers, William Starr and Newton, Walter H. The Hoover Administration. New York: Scribners, 1936.

Pemberton, William E. Bureaucratic Politics: Executive Reorganization During the Truman Administration. Columbia, Missouri: University of Missouri Press, 1979.

Polenberg, Richard. Reorganizing Roosevelt's Government: The Controversy Over Executive Reorganization, 1936-1939. Cambridge: Harvard University Press, 1966.

Rasmussen, Wayne D., and Baker, Gladys L. The Department of Agriculture. New York: Praeger, 1972.

Redford, Emmette S. and Marlan Blisett. Organizing the Executive Branch: The Johnson Presidency. Chicago: University of Chicago Press, 1981.

Seidman, Harold. Politics, Position, and Power: The Dynamics of Organization. 3d ed. New York: Oxford University Press, 1980.

Short, Lloyd M. The Development of National Administrative Organization in the United States. Baltimore: Johns Hopkins Press, 1923.

Simon, Herbert. Administrative Behavior: A Study of Decisionmaking Processes in Administrative Organization. 3d ed. New York: Free Press, c1976.

Smithies, Arthur. The Budgetary Process in the United States. New York: McGraw-Hill Book Company, 1955.

Somers, Herman Miles. Presidential Agency: OWMR, the Office of War Mobilization and Reconversion. Cambridge: Harvard University Press, 1950.

Szanton, Peter, ed. Federal Reorganization: What Have We Learned? Chatham, New Jersey: Chatham House Publishers, 1981.

Truman, Harry S. Memoirs: Years of Decision. v. 1. Garden City, New York: Doubleday and Company, 1955.

U.S. Commission on Organization of the Executive Branch of the Government (1947-1949). The Hoover Commission Report on Organization of the Executive Branch of the Government. New York: McGraw-Hill, 1949.

U.S. Congress. Senate. Committee on Governmental Affairs. The Federal Executive Establishment: Evolution and Trends. [by Ronald C. Moe] (Committee print) 96th Cong., 2d sess. Washington, U.S. Govt. Print. Off., 1980.

134

Waldo, Dwight. The Administrative State: A Study of the Political Theory of American Public Administration. New York: Ronald Press, 1948.

Wallace, Schuyler C. Federal Departmentalization: A Critique of Theories of Organization. New York: Columbia University Press, 1941.

Weber, Gustavus. Organized Efforts for the Improvement of Methods of Administration in the United States. New York: D. Appleton and Company, 1919.

White, Leonard D. Introduction to the Study of Public Administration. 4th rev. ed. New York: Macmillan Company, 1955.

Wilbur, Ray Lyman, and Hyde, Arthur M. The Hoover Policies. New York: Charles Scribner's Sons, 1937.

Willoughby, W. F. The Reorganization of the Administrative Branch of the National Government. Baltimore: Johns Hopkins Press, 1923.

Wilson, Joan Hoff. Herbert Hoover: Forgotten Progressive. Boston: Little, Brown and Company, 1975.

Wissler, Richard H. Challenge to Action: The Life and Works of Robert L. Johnson. Privately published, 1964.

Wolanin, Thomas R. Presidential Advisory Commissions: Truman to Nixon. Madison, University of Wisconsin Press, 1975.

ARTICLES

Aiken, Charles. "Task Force: Methodology." Public Administration Review 19 (Autumn 1949): 241-251.

Appleby, Paul H. "The Significance of the Hoover Commission Report." Yale Review 39 (September 1949): 1-22.

Arnold, Peri. "The First Hoover Commission and the Managerial Presidency." Journal of Politics 38 (February 1976): 46-70.

_____. "The 'Great Engineer' as Administrator: Herbert Hoover and Modern Bureaucracy." Review of Politics 42 (July 1980): 329-348.

_____. "Herbert Hoover and the Continuity of Public Policy." Public Policy 20 (Fall 1972): 525-544.

Arnold, Peri. "Reorganization and Politics: A Reflection on the Adequacy of Administrative Theory." Public Administration Review 34 (May-June 1974): 205-211.

Ash, Roy L. "Why the Federal Government Needs Restructuring." Fortune 83 (March 1971): 64-66.

Bernstein, Marver H. "Independent Regulatory Agencies: A Perspective on Their Reform." In The Government as a Regulator. Annals of the American Academy of Political and Social Science, 1972, v. 400: 14-26.

Degler, Carl. "The Ordeal of Herbert Hoover." Yale Review 52 (Summer 1963): 563-583.

Dimock, Marshall F. "Government Corporations: A Focus of Policy and Administration." Part I. American Political Science Review 43 (October 1949): 899-921.

Divine, William R. "Second Hoover Commission Reports--An Analysis." Public Administration Review 15 (Autumn 1955): 263--269.

Fesler, James. "Administrative Literature and the Second Hoover Commission." American Political Science Review 51 (March 1957): 135-157.

Finer, Herman. "The Hoover Commission Reports." Political Science Quarterly 64 (September 1949): 405-419.

Fisher, Louis and Moe, Ronald C. "Presidential Reorganization Authority: Is It Worth the Cost?" Political Science Quarterly 96 (Summer 1981): 301-318.

Gulick, Luther. "War Organization and the Federal Government." American Political Science Review 60 (April 1944): 1166-1179.

Hammond, Paul Y. "The National Security Council as a Device for Interdepartmental Coordination: An Interpretation and Appraisal." American Political Science Review 54 (December 1960): 899-910.

Hawley, Ellis W. "Herbert Hoover, the Commerce Secretariat, and the Vision of the Associative State, 1921-1928." The Journal of American History, 61 (June 1974): 116-140.

Heady, Ferrel. "A New Approach to Federal Executive Reorganization." American Political Science Review 41 (December 1947): 1118-1125.

_____ "The Operation of a Mixed Commission." American Political Science Review, 43 (October 1949): 940-952.

_____ "The Reorganization Act of 1949." Public Administration Review, 9 (Summer 1949): 165-174.

Heady, Ferrel.   "The Reports of the Hoover Commission." Review of
   Politics 11 (July 1949): 335-378.

Hoover, Herbert.   "We Can Cooperate and Yet Compete." Nation's Business 14 (June 15, 1926): 11-14.

Kaufman, Herbert.   "Reflections on Administrative Reorganization."
   In Setting National Priorities: the 1978 Budget. Joseph A.
   Pechman, ed. Washington: Brookings Institution (1977): 391-418.

Kennedy, Frank R.   "The American Medical Association: Power, Purpose,
   and Politics in Organized Medicine." Yale Law Journal 63
   (May 1954): 938-1022.

Koenig, Louis. ed.   "The Hoover Commissions: A Symposium." American Political Science Review 33 (October 1949): 933-1000.

Kraines, Oscar.   "The Cockrell Committee, 1887-1889: First Comprehensive Congressional Investigation in Administration." Western
   Political Quarterly 4 (December 1951): 583-609.

_____   "The President Versus Congress: The Keep Commission,
   1905-1909, First Comprehensive Presidential Inquiry in Administration." Western Political Quarterly 23 (March 1970): 5-54.

Maass, Arthur.   "Congress and Water Resources." American Political
   Science Review 44 (September 1950): 576-592.

Mansfield, Harvey C.   "Federal Executive Reorganization: Thirty
   Years of Experience." Public Administration Review 29 (July-
   August 1969): 332-345.

_____   "Reorganizing the Federal Executive Branch: The Limits of
   Institutionalization." Law and Contemporary Problems 25 (Summer
   1970): 461-495.

Millett, John D. and Rogers, Lindsay.   "The Legislative Veto and the
   Reorganization Act of 1939." Public Administration Review 1
   (Winter 1941): 176-189.

Musolf, Lloyd D. and Seidman, Harold.   "The Blurred Boundaries of
   Public Administration." Public Administration Review 40 (March/
   April 1980): 124-130.

Noggle, Burl.   "The Twenties: A New Historiographical Frontier."
   Journal of American History 53 (September 1966): 299-314.

Pritchett, C. Herman.   "The Regulatory Commissions Revisited."
   American Political Science Review 43 (October 1949): 978-989.

Sander, Alfred D.   "Truman and the National Security Council: 1945-
   1947." The Journal of American History 59 (September 1972):
   369-388.

Sayre, Wallace. "Premises of Public Administration: Past and
    Emerging." Public Administration Review 18 (Spring 1958): 102-
    105.

Schapsmeier, Edward L. and Frederick H.   "Disharmony in the Harding
    Cabinet." Ohio History 75 (Spring/Summer 1966): 126-136, 188-
    190.

Seidman, Harold.   "Government-Sponsored Enterprises in the United
    States." In The New Political Economy: The Public Use of the
    Private Sector. Bruce L.R. Smith, ed. New York: Macmillan Com-
    pany, (1975): p. 83-108.

_____   "The Government Corporation: Organization and Controls."
    Public Administration Review 14 (Summer 1954): 183-192.

_____   "The Theory of the Autonomous Government Corporation: A
    Critical Appraisal." Public Administration Review 12 (Spring
    1952): 89-96.

Sims, Lewis B.   "Improving Federal Management Services, Personnel."
    American Political Science Review 43 (October 1949): 990-993.

Stewart, J. Harold.   "The Hoover Commission Recommendations on Bud-
    get and Accounting." The Federal Accountant 7 (March 1958): 8-
    10.

"Summary of 'Reports of the Hoover Commission.'"   Public Adminis-
    tration Review 9 (Spring 1949): 73-99.

DOCUMENTS

There are a vast number of public documents related to the two
Hoover Commissions. Regarding the actual Commission and task force
reports and documents, the most readily accessible index is to be
found in: U.S., Congress, House, Committee on Government Operations,
Summary of the Objectives, Operations, and Results of the Commissions
on Organization of the Executive Branch of the Government (First and
Second Hoover Commissions) (Committee print), 88th Cong., 1st sess.,
1963.

Three status reports are particularly useful as guides to actions taken by the President and Congress on implementing the recommendations of the two Commissions. With respect to the first Commission, consult: (1) U.S., Congress, Senate, Reorganization of the Federal Government: Status of the Hoover Commission Reports, With List
of Public Laws Enacted, Reorganization Plans Approved or Disapproved,
and Bills Presently Pending to Effectuate Remaining Commission

(continued) Recommendations, (S. Doc. 91), 82d Cong., 2d sess.,
1952. (2) U.S., Congress., Senate., Committee on Government Operations, Senate Action on Hoover Commission Reports, (Committee
print), 82d Cong., 2d sess., 1958.

With respect to the second Commission, consult: U.S., Congress,
Senate, Committee on Government Operations, Action By the Congress
and the Executive Branch of the Government on the Second Hoover Commission Report, 1955-1957, (S. Rept. 1289), 85th Cong., 2d sess.,
1958.

A document useful to the first Commission was provided by W.
Brooke Graves of the Legislative Reference Service, Library of Congress. The full citation is: U.S., Library of Congress, Legislative
Reference Service, A Compilation of Basic Information on the Reorganization of the Executive Branch of the Government of the United
States, 1912-1947. [by W. Brooke Graves] [Mimeograph] Washington,
1947.

It is a rare Congress in which bills to create a new Hoover Commission are not introduced. Prior to 1981, the closest consideration
given a bill to create a commission occurred in 1968 when lengthy
hearings were conducted by the Senate Government Operations Committee
chaired by Senator Abraham Ribicoff. U.S., Congress, Senate, Committee on Government Operations, Establish a Commission on the Organization and Management of the Executive Branch (Modernizing the Government), Hearings, 90th Cong., 2d sess., 1968.

In 1981, Senators William Roth, Chairman of the Governmental Affairs Committee and Thomas Eagleton, ranking Minority Member of the
Committee, introduced S. 10 while an identical bill, H.R. 18, was introduced in the House by Representative Richard Bolling, Chairman of
the Rules Committee. Hearings were held on April 28 and May 20,
1981, by the Senate Governmental Affairs Committee and the Committee
reported the bill favorably on August 13, 1981. The Senate approved
the bill, as amended, on December 7, 1981, by a vote of 79-4.

(1) U.S., Congress, Senate, Committee on Governmental Affairs,
     Commission on More Effective Government, Hearings, 97th
     Cong., 1st sess., 1981.

(2) U.S., Congress, Senate, Committee on Governmental Affairs,
     To Establish a Commission on More Effective Government,
     (S. Rept. 97-179), 97th Cong., 1st sess., 1981.